D1613913

Sergeant Gander

Regimental Mascot
GANDER

A. Mainman
2005

A portrait of Sergeant Gander by artist Anne Mainman.

SERGEANT GANDER

A Canadian Hero

ROBYN
WALKER

NATURAL HERITAGE BOOKS
A MEMBER OF THE DUNDURN GROUP
TORONTO

Editor: Cheryl Hawley
Design: Courtney Horner
Printer: Marquis

Library and Archives Canada Cataloguing in Publication

Walker, Robyn, 1969-
      Sergeant Gander : a Canadian hero / by Robyn Walker.

Includes bibliographical references and index.
ISBN 978-1-55488-463-6

            1. Sergeant Gander (Dog)--Juvenile literature. 2. Canada. Canadian Army.
Royal Rifles of Canada--Mascots--Juvenile literature. 3. Dickin Medal--
Juvenile literature. 4. Newfoundland dogs--Juvenile literature. 5. Mascots--
Canada--Biography--Juvenile literature. I. Title.

D810.A65W35 2009   j940.54'251250929   C2009-903265-1

1   2   3   4   5   13   12   11   10   09

Conseil des Arts du Canada
Canada Council for the Arts

Canadä

ONTARIO ARTS COUNCIL
CONSEIL DES ARTS DE L'ONTARIO

We acknowledge the support of the **Canada Council for the Arts** and the **Ontario Arts Council** for our publishing program. We also acknowledge the financial support of the **Government of Canada** through the **Book Publishing Industry Development Program** and **The Association for the Export of Canadian Books**, and the **Government of Ontario** through the **Ontario Book Publishers Tax Credit program**, and the **Ontario Media Development Corporation**.

Care has been taken to trace the ownership of copyright material used in this book. The author and the publisher welcome any information enabling them to rectify any references or credits in subsequent editions.

J. Kirk Howard, President

Printed and bound in Canada.
Printed on recycled paper.
www.dundurn.com

Published by Natural Heritage Books
A Member of The Dundurn Group

Front Cover Photo: The Royal Rifles with Gander in Vancouver, British Columbia, October 27, 1941. *Courtesy of the National Archives of Canada PA-116791.*

Dundurn Press	Gazelle Book Services Limited	Dundurn Press
3 Church Street, Suite 500	White Cross Mills	2250 Military Road
Toronto, Ontario, Canada	High Town, Lancaster, England	Tonawanda, NY
M5E 1M2	LA1 4XS	U.S.A. 14150

Table of Contents

Acknowledgements

First and foremost, I must acknowledge the invaluable assistance of Jeremy Swanson, former Commemorations Officer at the Canadian War Museum, without whom there would be no Gander story. He provided a wealth of background information and first-hand accounts about Gander and the veterans themselves, and was unfailing in his willingness to assist in "getting the Gander story out there." It was never too late or too early to contact him and his replies were always quick and on point. The Gander story is his passion, and as a writer I benefited immensely from his willingness to share.

The assistance of the Hong Kong Veterans' Commemorative Association (HKVCA) has been immeasurable, with specific thanks to Jim Trick and Derrill Henderson. Their willingness to answer questions and provide resources is much appreciated. The incredible website of the HKVCA is a repository of information about the Battle of Hong Kong that is without equal. Thanks also to Isabel George and Gill Hubbard of the Peoples' Dispensary for Sick Animals, for their help in obtaining photographs and information about other animal war heroes.

Many thanks to Ron Parker and his fabulous website (dedicated to his father, Major Maurice Parker, Royal Rifles of Canada), which provides a wealth of personal accounts of the battle. Also to Eileen Elms, who was willing to share her childhood memories of "Pal" and of what it was like living in Gander, Newfoundland, back in 1941.

Many, many thanks to all of those individuals who provided photographs and photograph permissions for this book. Their willingness to share has truly enhanced this project.

Much appreciation goes out to Corinna Austin, one of the most talented "undiscovered" writers I know, and my personal muse. The moral support you provide me with on a daily basis means the world.

I would also like to thank my husband and son (Terry and Jed Walker) who supported my writing efforts; Jane Gibson and Barry Penhale at Natural Heritage Books, A Member of the Dundurn Group, for their belief in this project; and Sarah and Samantha, who were there every step of the way.

Foreword

To say that I was pleased to be asked to write the foreword to this book would be an understatement; it meant so much more to me than the reader could possibly understand. It was a highly satisfying personal honour, due to the extraordinary events that took place when the Gander story came to light.

While I was the commemorations and programs officer at the Canadian War Museum I took on several high-profile projects that resulted in major nationally and internationally recognized events. The Gander project was brought to my desk at the same time as several others, when things were the busiest and most stressful. My two volunteer researchers, Professor Howard Stutt (retired) and Second World War D-Day veteran George Shearman, were already heavily involved in different aspects on several projects at the time. My office and my staff were also actively engaged in the commemorations program to celebrate and mark the fiftieth anniversary of both VE day in May 1995, and VJ day in August 1995.

We were very thin on the ground and there was precious little time or resources to spare for something new. It was an exhausting program for us all, with meetings and events that seemed to happen every second or third day. In the middle of all of that there were research projects for the posthumous award of the Polish Home Army Cross to twenty-six Royal Canadian Air Force (RCAF) aircrew by the Polish government killed in action over Poland in 1940–45 (1996), and the commemoration of the heroic act of Perth resident Howard Stokes in saving the life of a young Dutch boy in 1945 (1997).

All of those projects would eventually have highly successful outcomes, but at that particular moment their completion seemed impossible. Into the midst of this frantic activity came the dog Gander. He came to my attention in the strangest of ways; many people have since remarked that it seemed to have been pre-ordained. Whatever it was that made it happen, it was certainly at the most appropriate of times.

The Canadian government had introduced the long overdue "Hong Kong" clasp to the CVSM (the Canadian Volunteer Service Medal), a general service medal for veterans of the Hong Kong Battle of December 8 to 25, 1941, on July 2, 1995. The first presentations of the new bar were made by Veterans Affairs in Ottawa on August 11, 1995, as part of the VJ Day fiftieth anniversary.

At the ceremony I was accompanying the family of Canada's first Victoria Cross winner, Sergeant Major John Osborn of Winnipeg, who was killed at Hong Kong in the selfless act of saving several of his men by throwing himself on a hand grenade. The family were the guests of the Canadian War Museum as they had donated the medal to the Museum, and I was tasked with looking after them during their stay in Ottawa.

At the social gathering after the medals award ceremony I was gathered with a group of Hong Kong veterans from both the Royal Rifles of Canada and Winnipeg Grenadiers, and the family of John Osborn. We were discussing the medals and the courage of Sergeant Major Osborn. I made a casual remark to the assembled guests that it must have taken tremendous courage and immediate instinctive reaction to have performed such a deed with a deadly smoking hand grenade just feet away, waiting to deliver death and destruction to many.

One of the veterans near me, who I believe was Bob Manchester of the Winnipeg Grenadiers, answered my statement by replying "Yes. Just like that damn dog." In answer to my immediate question, Bob Manchester and his friend Robert "Flash" Clayton told me all about Gander and what he had done. I shall never forget it; I was stunned by what I heard. I had heard many stories about the battles in Hong Kong, and indeed in many other wars, but never one about a dog picking up a grenade in the middle of battle. That night Manchester told me that he and his comrades had always felt that the dog deserved a medal for what he had done in saving the lives of seven wounded men, but that in the aftermath of war and history no one wanted to know about a dog mascot. Still, they kept hoping it would happen. And so it has.

So that night in August 1995, Gander, the beloved dog mascot of the Royal Rifles of Canada, entered the story and my life. It was the start of three years of dedicated work by my volunteer group and office staff to find out what had happened, research all the evidence, and present the story to the People's Dispensary for Sick Animals (PDSA) in the United Kingdom for eligibility for the award of the Dickin Medal, known as the "Animals' Victoria Cross."

For me, one of the most poignant moments came at the end of August when Roger Cyr, past president of the Hong Kong Veterans' Association (HKVA), sat in front of me in my office at the War Museum and told me the story of Gander from the point of view of the men who were there and knew him. Roger told the story with difficulty because he had to tell me about the regiment's battle at the same time. He burst into tears in the middle of it and said to me through his tears, "Jeremy don't ever let them forget us!" I have always felt that in this meeting, in the moment of tearful memory while he told the story of Gander, he was also telling me the story of the men he served with, and that somehow by recognizing Gander's bravery perhaps we could all remember the courage of the men who fought, died, and endured unspeakable horrors at Hong Kong, so many years before. It seemed that Gander's recognition would help the generations that follow to understand and recognize what the soldiers had done.

Roger Cyr was a wise man, as well as a brave one. It would not have been easy to deny a request from a man with such heart and soul. That afternoon I promised him that I would do what he had asked. I did not let him down. It took three years to complete, but we did it. Roger was there at the award ceremony. I am sure I saw a glint in his eye and a wink of thanks as he presented me a life membership in the Hong Kong Veterans' Association in October 2000, in recognition of my work for Gander and the Association.

What took place between the moment of Gander's story being revealed and the awarding of the Dickin Medal is contained within this fine book by Robyn Walker. It is a fascinating tale. I have never asked Robyn how she learned of Gander, or why she wanted to do the book, but in meeting with her I did know that it was going to be a good one and that the story would be complete, which it has proved to be. In reading this book I have been immensely gratified to learn so many things about the Gander story that my volunteers and office group did not know at the time. I realize now that there were many "blanks" in the narrative and many unanswered questions over the years, which time and events did not allow us to understand, but now we have them all gathered here, in Robyn's book.

This is a wonderful story that will ensure that Gander's story will be remembered in Canadian history for all time. As a result of this book, and Robyn Walker's impeccable research and hard work, I hope that generations of children will learn about Gander and come face to face with Canadian history, in particular with the history of the veterans of Hong Kong. The late Roger Cyr and Bob Manchester would be pleased. Roger would surely agree that his tearful moment with me, over a decade ago, was worth it for him, his comrades, and for their mascot who has been recognized at last. Let this book, and the story of the brave and wonderful Gander, serve as a literary memorial to them all and a testament to their collective courage. All because of that "damn dog."

So now we have had the recognition of the veterans and the medal for Gander, and now we have the story in print. I hope to live to see a statue of Gander erected in Ottawa, so that Canadian children and visitors will ask about it, and learn about the extraordinary Canadian men who fought at Hong Kong in extraordinary times. It is a heroic tale indeed.

Jeremy Swanson
Ottawa, Ontario

Introduction

Grenade! A group of Canadian soldiers stare in terror at the small but deadly object that has landed among them. Are the soldiers doomed? Are they destined to die on a dirty, dusty Hong Kong road, thousands of kilometres away from home? Only an act of tremendous courage and selflessness can save the young Canadian soldiers. Suddenly one of their comrades darts forward, ready to make the ultimate sacrifice.

The Battle of Hong Kong

France and Great Britain declared war on Germany on September 3, 1939; the Second World War was formally underway. Under the leadership of Adolf Hitler[1], Germany had been steadily overpowering its weaker neighbours, such as Austria and Czechoslovakia, and when Germany invaded Poland on September 1, 1939, both Great Britain and France finally realized that only military intervention might stop Nazi Germany from taking over all of Europe.

However, in the year that followed Germany seemed unstoppable. In April 1940, Norway and Denmark fell to the Germans. On May 10, 1940, the Germans launched a massive attack against the Netherlands and Belgium. In less than a month the Germans had pushed into France, pinning the British Expeditionary Force that had been stationed there against the sea. While many of the British troops were evacuated across the English Channel, France itself surrendered to the Germans on June 22, 1940. Britain now stood alone in Europe against the powerful German forces.

In Asia, Japan was also looking to expand its empire. Japan invaded China in 1937, and in November 1940, signed a pact aligning itself with Germany and

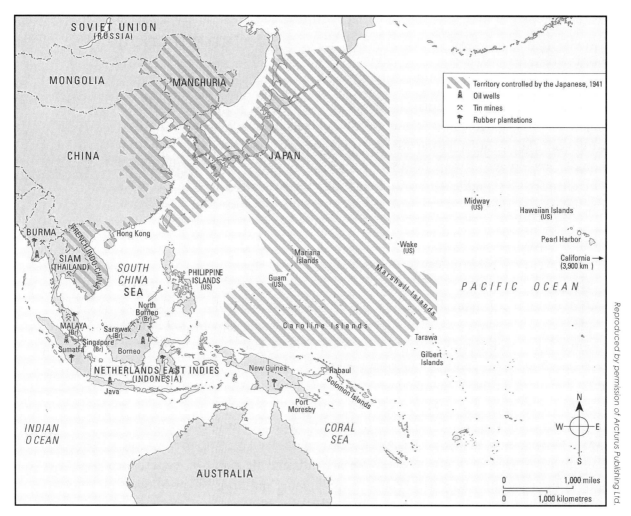

Southeast Asia, 1940.

Italy. This alliance allowed Japan to put pressure on the Dutch (who were under German occupation) to sell more oil to Japan from their East Indian oil reserves.[2] Vichy France,[3] whose government was, in fact, controlled by the Germans, was pressured into allowing Japanese troops to be stationed in French Indochina. The influx of Japanese troops and aircraft into Indochina posed a very real threat to the

SERGEANT GANDER

British colonies of Burma, Hong Kong, and Malaya, and to the British naval base at Singapore. Britain knew that her Asian colonies were vulnerable to Japanese attack, but most of the British military strength was focused on the war in Europe. Therefore, the British asked Canada to help them defend their colonies in Asia.

The Canadians agreed to help their British ally. Canada had already demonstrated their solidarity with Britain by declaring war on Germany on September 10, 1939, and was already sending a steady stream of war materials and soldiers to support Britain. The Canadian navy patrolled the Atlantic sea lanes, protecting the convoys of supplies being sent from North America, and Canadian pilots and soldiers were being recruited and trained to help in the fight against Germany. When asked to assist in defending the Hong Kong colony against possible Japanese aggression, Canada agreed to send two infantry battalions to the island to help reinforce the British garrison that was stationed there. During the autumn of 1941, two Canadian units, the Royal Rifles of Canada and the Winnipeg Grenadiers, departed for Hong Kong.

Less than a month after the Canadians' arrival in Hong Kong, the Japanese launched their attack against the colony. The Canadians fought bravely, but could not withstand the Japanese onslaught and in less than three weeks the colony of Hong Kong was completely overrun. The British and Canadian troops surrendered to the Japanese on Christmas Day 1941, and were dispatched to Japanese prisoner of war camps for the remainder of the war. Those who survived the horrific conditions of the camps and returned to Canada at the end of the war helped to form the Hong Kong Veterans' Association of Canada. They continue to work hard to preserve the memory of their fallen comrades.

Of all the Canadians who participated in the Battle of Hong Kong, only one was awarded the PDSA Dickin Medal. This medal is awarded to animals that display gallantry and devotion to duty while under the control of any branch of the armed forces. Sergeant Gander is the nineteenth dog ever to receive this medal, and the first Canadian canine to do so. This is his story.

List of Maps

SERGEANT GANDER

1: Bear on the Runway

Gander, a purebred Newfoundland dog, was born in the Dominion of Newfoundland, most likely in 1939. His family, the Haydens, had named him "Pal." Newfoundland dogs are enormous animals, with long, shaggy black fur, known for their love of children, swimming skills, and rescuing abilities. As a puppy, Pal had a voracious appetite and grew rapidly. His intelligence and good temperament made him easy to train, and he enjoyed spending much of his time out of doors. Pal was well-known to the members of the small local community and was a much loved family pet. Certainly no one could have predicted that the small but growing bundle of black fur would one day be considered a war hero!

Gander, Newfoundland, was selected as the site for the construction of an airport due to its location near the northeastern tip of the North American continent. Construction began in 1936, and the town started to develop. In 1940, Gander was not so much a town as a collection of construction camps. There were very few civilians living there and only about ten homes had been built. When the one-room schoolhouse opened, it had only fourteen pupils. Rod Hayden, his wife, and his young son Jack were one of the few families living there. Rod Hayden was the depot officer for the Shell Oil Company, and Gander Airport was a major refilling station for planes that were on their way to England.

In July 1940, the Germans had launched a massive bombing campaign against England in preparation for the invasion of the island nation. British factories, airfields, and cities were the targets of the German bombers. The Royal Air Force (RAF) fighter pilots sustained heavy casualties in defence of their homeland, and the supply of replacement pilots could not keep pace with the losses. To help bolster the RAF numbers, many pilots were trained in Canada and then sent over to England, where they defended England's skies against German bombers or engaged in bombing missions themselves against German targets.[5]

Description of Newfoundland Dogs

Newfoundland dogs are massive animals, with males measuring over seventy centimetres in height and weighing just over sixty-seven kilograms. The females measure about sixty-one centimetres and weigh about fifty-four kilograms. Their thick black

Photograph of a Newfoundland dog.

coats (sometimes mixed with white, solid brown, or grey) are water repellent, and their feet are webbed, making them excellent swimmers. The breed is described by the United Kennel Club in Kalamazoo, Michigan, as, "Possessing natural life saving instincts. Their gentle expression reflects the benevolence, intelligence, and dignity that are breed characteristics."[1] The rescue instinct, innate in Newfoundlands, is so respected that the breed was considered, "required lifesaving equipment," along the coast of England during the 1800s.[2] Newfoundland dogs are now widely used as therapy dogs, in search and rescue missions, and as water rescue dogs.

Two of the world's most famous writers have penned their own observations of the Newfoundland dog. The British poet Lord Byron, pining after the death of his own Newfoundland dog Boatswain, wrote a poem called "Epitaph to a Dog," which reads:

> *Near this spot*
> *Are deposited the remains*
> *Of one*
> *Who possessed Beauty*

Without Vanity,
Strength without Insolence,
Courage without Ferocity,
And all the Virtues of Man,
Without his Vices.

This Praise, which would be unmeaning Flattery
If inscribed over Human Ashes,
Is but a just tribute to the Memory of
"Boatswain," a Dog. [3]

American philosopher-naturalist Henry David Thoreau, in his book Walden, *simply states, "A man is not a good man to me because he will feed me if I should be starving, or warm me if I should be freezing, or pull me out of a ditch if I should ever fall in one. I can find you a Newfoundland dog that will do as much."*[4]

Sergeant Gander's heroism may be Canada's highest profile Newfoundland rescue story, but throughout Canadian history there have been many more. Two examples are the stories of Tang and Hairy Dog:

> *Tang: In 1919, a ship called the* Ethie *ran aground just off the coast of western Newfoundland. Tang, the ship's massive Newfoundland dog, jumped into the sea and swam to shore with a rope in his mouth. People on shore secured the rope and used it to rescue the members of the* Ethie*'s crew. Tang received a medal from the Lloyd's of London insurance company for his heroic deed.*
>
> *Hairy Dog: In 1832 the* Despatch, *a ship carrying over 150 Irish immigrants, wrecked just off the coast of Newfoundland. The Harvey family, from Isle aux Morts (Island of Death), saw the wreck and had their pet Newfoundland, Hairy Dog, swim out to the survivors and help tow them ashore.*

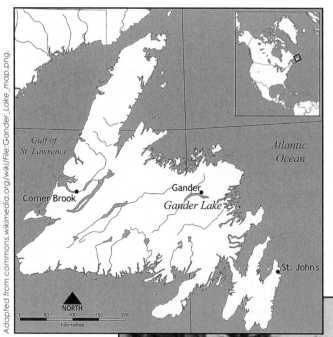

Location of
Gander in
Newfoundland.

From the time that Pal was a pup he became actively involved in the Canadian war effort. In 1940, the Dominion of Newfoundland gave operating control of Gander Airport to the Royal Canadian Air Force (RCAF). Renamed RCAF Station Gander in 1941, the airport became a hub of military activity as it was used not only as a disembarkation centre for pilots, but also for the transport of newly built aircraft from North America to the European war theatre. The airport was also a staging area for anti-submarine patrols. Pal was a familiar figure at the airport. When he was old enough he

Gander/Pal
with an un-
identified male
friend, winter
1940.

SERGEANT GANDER

was often put to work, harnessed to haul fifty-gallon drums of petrol, two at a time, from the warehouse to the airplanes to assist in the refuelling process. In fact, Pal is affectionately remembered as the first refuelling "vehicle" at the Gander airport.

When Pal wasn't working he enjoyed racing around the airfield and taking naps right on the landing strips. For pilots, the large dog presented a huge problem. He was so big and shaggy that many pilots radioed in that they couldn't land because there was a bear on the runway. Eileen Elms (formerly Chafe), a local Gander schoolgirl, remembers "Douglas Fraser, who landed the first plane here, did say he saw what he thought was a bear on the taxiway and it turned out to be Pal."[6]

A Brief History of Newfoundland and Labrador

The territory known as Newfoundland and Labrador is made up of the island of Newfoundland and the area named Labrador, which is located on the continental mainland of Canada. Newfoundland and Labrador are situated on the northeastern side of North America, on the Atlantic Ocean. Originally populated by indigenous people, Newfoundland was also home to several short-lived Viking settlements as early as 986 AD. Rediscovered by the Europeans approximately five hundred years later, it was first claimed for England by explorer John Cabot in 1497, and later by Sir Humphrey Gilbert in 1583. Newfoundland was a British colony up until 1907, when it acquired self-government status and was renamed the Dominion of Newfoundland.

Hit hard by the Great Depression of the late 1920s and early 1930s, the Newfoundland government asked the British to take back control of Newfoundland in 1934, until the Dominion could become more self-sustaining. Between 1934 and 1949 a six member Commission of Government was responsible for the administration of Newfoundland, reporting directly to London. After the war two referendums were held to determine the fate of Newfoundland. The first, in 1946, was inconclusive, with 44.5 per cent of Newfoundlanders supporting

Canada and Newfoundland showing territorial boundaries as of 1941 (created in 1915).

the restoration of Dominion status, 41.4 per cent supporting confederation with Canada, and 14.3 per cent supporting the continuation of the Commission of Government.[7] The second referendum, held in 1949, offered only two choices: restoration of Dominion status or confederation with Canada. With fifty-two per cent of the vote supporting Confederation, Newfoundland became Canada's tenth province on March 31, 1949.

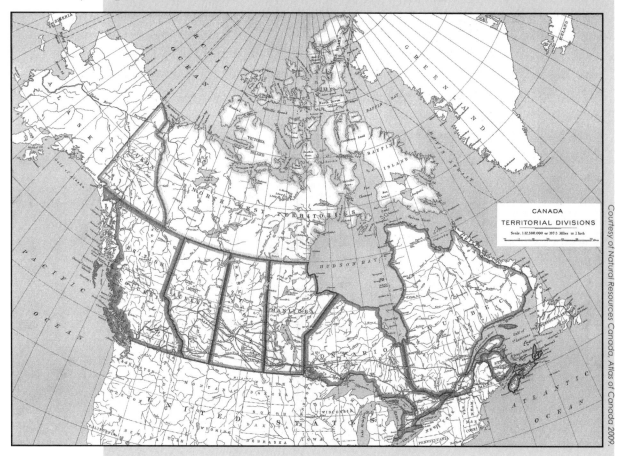

SERGEANT GANDER

Gander Airport to 1945

Construction of the airport at Gander began in 1936, and it became operational two years later. With four paved runways it was the world's largest airport at the time, and was known as Newfoundland Airport.

In 1941, with the war raging in Europe and the German threat growing, the Newfoundland government offered control of the airport to the Canadian government. The strategic importance of this airport had caught the attention of both the Canadian and Newfoundland governments. It was North America's most easterly land-based airport, making it an ideal refuelling point for trans-Atlantic flights. Its location also gave pilots the greatest range for surveillance flights over the western Atlantic Ocean. However, there were fears that the airport, which had no active defence force, might fall into the hands of the Germans. The Newfoundland governor, Sir Humphrey Walwyn, requested that the facility be turned over to Canada for the duration of the war.

The Canadian government agreed and Royal Canadian Air Force (RCAF) bombers arrived at the airport in June 1940, followed soon after by soldiers from Canada's Black Watch, a reserve military unit from Montreal, Quebec. The Black Watch regiment and the RCAF's orders were to defend the airport from air attacks or sea-based landings, and to patrol the western Atlantic to provide early warning of any enemy attack. The airport was renamed RCAF Gander, and expansion began almost immediately with additional hangars, barracks, and storage being added to the existing facility. The German threat to Canada's eastern coastline proved to be very real. Not only did German submarines attack and sink Canadian ships, penetrating as far as Rimouski on the St. Lawrence River, but the Germans also laid mines in the waters off Halifax and St. John's and were able to establish an automatic weather station in Northern Labrador.

By November 1940, Ferry Command, a Royal Air Force Service that had been raised in status, was also operating out of RCAF Gander. Planes built in Canada and the United States for Britain's Royal Air Force (RAF) were "ferried" or flown across the Atlantic, as opposed to being dismantled and shipped by sea. This was a much faster means of getting the aircraft to Britain and less hazardous as well,

Courtesy of the National Archives of Canada PA-116995.

Photograph of Canadian Prime Minister Mackenzie King at Gander Airport, August 1941.

since ships were always vulnerable to Gereman U-boat attack.

As the war progressed so did the activity at RCAF Gander. By the latter part of 1941, the air traffic was so heavy that more barracks and hangars had to be built, and the runways were lengthened. Service facilities like a bakery, a laundry, and a hospital were added. Also in 1941, the Americans were invited onto the base to assist in the war effort, although they had not yet formally entered the war. They stationed troops there and added their own facilities to the base, creating an "American side." By 1943, RCAF Gander was the largest air force base in Canada, playing such an important role in Ferry Command that Britain's Prime Minister Winston Churchill called RCAF Gander, "the largest aircraft carrier in the North Atlantic."[8] At the end of the war many of the troops and materials returning from Europe were also transported through the site.

RCAF Station Gander was disbanded in 1945, and control of the airport was returned to Newfoundland.

Despite the difficulties that Pal caused for incoming pilots, his friendly nature made him an extremely popular figure at the airport. Adored by the neighbourhood children, Pal was their constant playmate. He loved playing with them too, and even allowed himself to be harnessed up to pull their sleds in the winter. Pal liked to run fast and he would race across the hardpacked snow with the sled bouncing along behind him. He wasn't very good at stopping though, and the ride usually ended with the children toppling off the sled. Eileen Elms fondly recalls, "He was very playful and gentle with us children ... and often knocked us in the snow ... we all loved him."[9]

Pal loved to greet people by rearing up and placing his paws on their shoulders. But one day he jumped up on a little girl, Joan Chafe, and accidentally scratched her face. The injury to the girl's face was actually quite severe. Joan's sister, Eileen, who witnessed the accident recalled that day: "I was one of the children who played daily with Pal ... A photo of Pal hangs on my living room wall. He's harnessed to a sled and I'm one of the three children being pulled by the dog ... One day during play the dog jumped on my sister's shoulders, but his paw missed and accidentally scratched her face."[10] Eileen's sister had scratches in three places, and she remembers,

Photograph of Gander/ Pal pulling neighbourhood children Tom Hayden, Mike Ratcliffe, and Eileen Chafe.

Courtesy of Eileen Elms.

"There was lots of blood and both my mother and Mrs. Hayden were very upset … my sister had the scars 'til she died as there was no doctor to stitch her face, and it didn't seem serious — nor was it really."[11] Worried that Pal was becoming simply too big to be a family pet any longer, and that he was too much of a hazard to have running around the airfield, the Hayden family gave Pal to the Royal Rifles of Canada, an army regiment stationed at Gander Airport. The Royal Rifles, who had trained at Valcartier, Quebec, and who had previously been stationed in Sussex, New Brunswick, had arrived in Gander in November 1940. The majority of the Royal Rifles were stationed at Gander Airport while two companies were stationed at the Botwood seaport. The neighbourhood children were heartbroken, but the soldiers were ecstatic. The Royal Rifles renamed Pal "Gander," and the big dog went from being a much loved family pet, to a much loved army mascot.

Mackenzie King

William Lyon Mackenzie King was Canada's longest-serving prime minister. The grandson of William Lyon Mackenzie, leader of the Rebellion of 1837, King was selected by the Liberal Party as the successor to Sir Wilfred Laurier in 1920, and was elected prime minister in 1921. King had many years of experience in politics before being elected prime minister, including serving as the minister of labour under the Laurier government. He was a political science and law graduate from the University of Toronto, and also held degrees from the universities of Harvard and Chicago.

When the Second World War began in Europe, the Canadian government did not automatically commit itself to go to war on behalf of Great Britain. King was adamant that only the Canadian Parliament could decide upon a declaration of war. However, he felt that Canada did have an obligation to support Great Britain and following a special session of Parliament, held on September 7, 1939, King announced that "if this house will not support us in that policy, it will have to find some other government to assume the responsibilities of the present."[12] On September 10, 1939, after several days of debate in the House of Commons, Canada issued a formal declaration of war against Germany.

King was a staunch supporter of supplying aid to Great Britain throughout the war. He also provided a vital communications link between British Prime Minister Winston Churchill and American President Franklin Roosevelt, until the Americans formally entered the war in 1941. Throughout the war, King's government ensured the steady flow of war materials to Great Britain.

Mackenzie King was re-elected in 1945, just after the end of the war in Europe. He announced his retirement in 1948, having served twenty-two years as prime minister. He died of pneumonia on July 22, 1950, and is buried in Toronto at Mount Pleasant Cemetery.

Mackenzie King was also a dog lover. In July 1924, King was given an Irish Terrier puppy by some close friends. He named the dog Pat and the two became devoted companions. Daily walks and evenings sharing cookies and Ovaltine became part of the pair's regular routine. Pat was so important to King that the little dog was mentioned in almost every entry in his personal diary over the next seventeen years.

In due time, Pat became sick and died in July 1941, an event that caused King much sorrow. In his December 31, 1941, diary entry, King wrote, "As I think it all over tonight, the event that touched me most deeply of all was perhaps the death of little Pat. Our years together, and particularly our months in the early spring and summer, have been a true spiritual pilgrimage. That little dog has taught me how to live, and how to look forward, without concern, to the arms that will be around me when I too, pass away. We shall be together in the Beyond. Of that I am perfectly sure."[12]

The Rt. Hon. W.L. Mackenzie King with his dog Pat at Moorside Cottage, August 21, 1940.

Ferry Command

Ferry Command was created in response to the desperate need for airplanes to support the British war effort. British airplane factories were obvious targets for German bombers. In an effort to ensure a continuous supply of aircraft with which to defend itself, Britain looked to Canada and the United States to keep the Royal Air Force supplied. Recognizing that surface shipping over the Atlantic Ocean was very slow and very vulnerable to attack, the idea of having pilots "ferry" the planes across the ocean was developed.

However, the plan found little support among RAF commanders, who felt that the distance across the Atlantic was too far, and the weather too unpredictable for the idea to be worthwhile in practice. Moreover, the RAF couldn't spare any pilots to ferry the aircraft. Lord Beaverbrook, senior cabinet minister in Britain's government, ignored the RAF's concerns and set up an all-civilian organization to implement the operation. The ferrying program experienced success throughout the 1940s and early 1941, and by July 1941 it was taken over by the Royal Air Force. At that point, Air Chief Marshall Sir Frederick Bowhill was placed in charge of Ferry Command, and its primary function was to fly newly constructed aircraft from Canadian and American factories to operational units in Great Britain.

Its pilots were a mixed lot — crop dusters, barnstormers, bush pilots, and stunt pilots; Americans, Canadians, and a variety of Europeans. Few of the pilots had any trans-Atlantic experience, but all of them shared the courage to give it a try. The civilian ranks were often supplemented by recent graduates from the British Commonwealth Air Training Plan,[14] made up of pilots, navigators, wireless operators who wanted to gain some transatlantic flight experience, and experienced Royal Canadian Air Force pilots who were en route to assignments overseas. Gander Airport was used as the refuelling stop on the first ferry route. The success of the program meant that further routes were added. Smaller range planes could refuel in Goose Bay (Labrador), Greenland, and Iceland. There was also a South Route that linked the United States to Egypt. In March 1943, Ferry Command was subsumed into Transport Command, which had a global, as opposed to merely trans-Atlantic, operational area. Throughout the course of the war over 9,000 aircraft were ferried across the Atlantic.

SERGEANT GANDER

Royal Air Force Ferry Command, October 1941. Lockheed Hudson Mark IIIs are prepared for their trans-Atlantic ferry flights.

2: Sergeant Gander, Royal Rifles of Canada

Mobilized at Quebec City, in July 1940, the Royal Rifles of Canada drew most of their recruits from eastern Quebec and western New Brunswick. It was an English-speaking unit, but almost one quarter of the recruits were bilingual French Canadians. In the fall of 1940, the Royal Rifles were transferred to Sussex, New Brunswick, for further training, and by November they had been moved to Newfoundland. Their primary task there was to protect Gander Airport from German attack. They had been performing guard duty, combined with some training, for about six months when they acquired their regimental mascot, Sergeant Gander. As George MacDonell remembers, "…the regiment was presented with a purebred Newfoundland dog. He was jet black and looked more like a small pony than a dog. He was named Gander, after the airport. Gander was the biggest dog I had ever seen. He had a heavy, furry coat and webs between his toes, and could swim in the cold Atlantic like a walrus."

The Royal Rifles adored their new recruit. A handler, Fred Kelly, was assigned to Gander. Each day Kelly fed him, brushed him, and gave him a shower. Although Gander loved his daily shower, Kelly needed to be quick on his feet, because once Gander was finished, one big shake of his body was all that was needed to leave his handler soaking wet. Another one of Gander's tricks was to bolt outside after his shower and roll in the sand, leaving himself a filthy mess. Therefore, every effort was made to keep Gander inside until his coat had dried. Fred Kelly recalls, "Gander was no problem to look after. I had dogs all my life and we kind of took to each other right away. He ate anything and everything but had a particular taste for beer which he would drink out of the sink. He was a very playful dog and would often stop me in my tracks by resting his front paws on my shoulders."[2]

The Royal Rifles treated Gander like one of their own. Gander was given his own kitbag, just like the other soldiers, a kitbag that contained his blanket, brush, and food bowl. The soldiers even built Gander a doghouse, but he didn't like it very much. He howled and cried so much that Fred Kelly simply brought him inside the barracks and let him sleep on the floor beside his bed.

Gander appeared to be well aware of his importance in the regiment. Explains George MacDonell, "He was soon promoted to sergeant and wore his red stripes on a black leather harness with the regimental badge. He proudly strutted at the head of the band on church parades and … refused all other canines entry to the barracks."[3]

In May 1941, the Royal Rifles were transferred to St. John's, Newfoundland, to perform garrison duty and receive further training. By September 1941, the Royal Rifles had been moved back to Canada, and were stationed at Saint John, New Brunswick. At that point, the director of military training, Colonel John Lawson, identified the Royal Rifles as "insufficiently trained and not recommended for operations."[4] Despite his observation, a month later the Royal Rifles received their orders to prepare for overseas duty. Although their destination was unknown, the decision had been made that the Royal Rifles, along with the Winnipeg Grenadiers, would be sent to Hong Kong to help reinforce the British garrison against Japanese attack. The British had been hoping that the combination of Japan's military commitments in China, their fear of antagonizing the United States, and the threat of an attack by Soviet Russia on their northern borders, might deter Japan from attacking Britain's Asian colonies. However, when Japan signed a Neutrality Pact with the Soviet Union in April 1941, the British recognized the increased threat to their holdings in Asia. With Great Britain tied down defending their homeland from German attack, they needed all the help they could get to protect their colonies in other parts of the world.

The decision to reinforce the defences of Hong Kong was a contentious one. Both the British chiefs of staff and British Prime Minister Winston Churchill opposed any further strengthening of the colony. In August 1940, the chiefs of staff stated:

> Hong Kong is not a vital interest and the garrison could not withstand Japanese attack … Even if we had a strong fleet in the

Far East, it is doubtful that Hong Kong could be held now that the Japanese are firmly established on the mainland of China ... In the event of war, Hong Kong must be regarded as an outpost and held as long as possible. We should resist the inevitably strong pressure to reinforce Hong Kong and we should certainly be unable to relieve it.[5]

This sentiment was echoed by Churchill at the beginning of 1941, when he stated, "If Japan goes to war with us there is not the slightest chance of holding Hong Kong or relieving it. It is most unwise to increase the loss we shall suffer there. Instead of increasing the garrison it ought to be reduced to a symbolic scale ... We must avoid frittering away our resources on untenable positions. Japan will think long before declaring war on the British Empire and whether there are two or six battalions at Hong Kong will make no difference to her choice. I wish we had fewer troops there, but to move any of them would be noticeable and dangerous."[6]

Yet there was a faction, including Air Chief Marshall Sir Robert Brooke-Popham, Rear Admiral Sir Tom Phillips, and Major-General A.E. Grasett (commander of the Hong Kong Volunteer Defence Force), who believed that Hong Kong should be held. Grasett's appeal to the British War Office, suggesting that the Canadians might be willing to assist in the reinforcement of Hong Kong, found some receptive ears and in September 1941, a cable was sent to Ottawa, proposing that,

A small re-enforcement of the garrison of Hong Kong, e.g. by one or two battalions, would be very fully justified. It would increase the strength of the garrison out of all proportion to the actual numbers involved and it would provide a very strong stimulus to the garrison and to the Colony, it would further have a great moral effect in the whole of the Far East and would reassure Chiang Kai Shek as to the reality of our intent to hold the Island ... We should therefore be most grateful if the Canadian Government would consider whether one or two Canadian battalions could be provided from Canada for this purpose....[7]

The Canadian Cabinet War Committee met on September 23, 1941, to discuss the proposal and on October 2, 1941, Canada agreed to reinforce the Hong Kong garrison.

The Royal Rifles of Canada and the Winnipeg Grenadiers were selected for the mission. Canada's best trained units were classified as Class A and units that were not quite as far along in their training were labelled Class B. The remaining units, "due either to recent employment requiring a period of refresher training, or to insufficient training" that were "not recommended for operational employment at

The Winnipeg Grenadiers

The Winnipeg Grenadiers trace their origins back to 1908, and were one of the first units mobilized when Canada entered the Second World War. The Grenadiers were an English-speaking unit, recruited from western Canada. First designated as machine-gun unit, they completed basic training during the winter of 1939–40. In May 1940, they were converted to a rifle unit and sent to the island of Jamaica in the Caribbean to perform garrison duty. In Jamaica, the Grenadiers, like the Royal Rifles in Gander, adopted a dog as their mascot. Named "Queenie," the little dog was a favourite amongst the men. Winnipeg Grenadier William Bell recalls, "At some point while we were there, Queenie became pregnant. I remember one day when members of the regiment were on the way up the mountain near Newcastle and we all had to stop so that Queenie could have her puppies along the way. I don't know whatever happened to Queenie, but she was a good friend to many of us."[11]

After sixteen months in tropical Jamaica, the Grenadiers were recalled to Canada and told to prepare for service overseas. Like the Royal Rifles, the director of military training, Colonel John Lawson, had deemed the Grenadiers "insufficiently trained and not recommended for operations."[12]

Japanese Expansion

As early as 1931, when Japan seized control of Manchuria, their desire to win complete control over Eastern Asia and the Pacific was evident. In 1934–35, the Japanese began a rapid naval buildup (in violation of the Washington Naval Conferences of 1921–22[13] and later treaties) and in November 1936, Japan joined Germany in an Anti-Comintern Pact, which was ostensibly a defensive alliance against the spread of Communism.[14] On July 7, 1937, Japanese and Chinese troops clashed along the

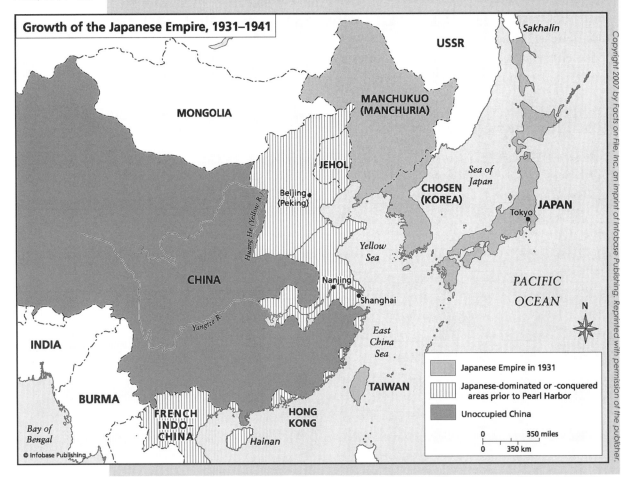

Growth of the Japanese Empire, 1931–1941

USSR

Sakhalin

MONGOLIA

MANCHUKUO
(MANCHURIA)

JEHOL

Beijing
(Peking)

Huang He (Yellow R.)

CHOSEN
(KOREA)

*Sea of
Japan*

Tokyo

JAPAN

*Yellow
Sea*

CHINA

Nanjing

Shanghai

*PACIFIC
OCEAN*

Yangtze R.

*East
China
Sea*

INDIA

TAIWAN

BURMA

*Bay of
Bengal*

FRENCH
INDO-
CHINA

HONG
KONG

Hainan

© Infobase Publishing

Japanese Empire in 1931

Japanese-dominated or -conquered areas prior to Pearl Harbor

Unoccupied China

0   350 miles

0   350 km

Chinese-Manchurian border. This skirmish led to full-scale war, and most historians refer to this as the start of the Second World War in Eastern Asia.

By 1938, the Japanese had penetrated deep into South China. In May of that year Japanese troops landed at Amoy, 483 kilometres northeast of Hong Kong, and by October they had landed troops at Bias Bay, only fifty-six kilometres northeast of the colony. Canton fell to the Japanese later that month and by early 1939 the Japanese occupied all of the territory adjacent to Hong Kong's mainland frontier.[15] In September 1940, the partnership between Germany and Japan (also including Italy) was further formalized with the signing of the Tripartite Pact, which stated,

> The Governments of Japan, Germany and Italy consider it the prerequisite of lasting peace that every nation in the world shall receive the space to which it is entitled. They have, therefore, decided to stand by and cooperate with one another in their efforts in the regions of Europe and Greater East Asia respectively. In doing this it is their prime purpose to establish and maintain a new order of things, calculated to promote the mutual prosperity and welfare of the peoples concerned....[16]

In other words, they intended to establish their own political and social agendas in their chosen geographic spheres of influence, by force if necessary.

As the war continued to rage in Europe, Japan was adding to its conquests in Asia. In July 1941, Japanese troops occupied French Indochina, an act that elicited a strong response from the United States. President Roosevelt ordered all Japanese assets in America frozen and placed an embargo on the shipment of goods to Japan. Japan retaliated by freezing American assets in Japanese controlled territories, and trade between the two nations effectively came to a standstill. Britain, preoccupied with the war in Europe, could do little in response to Japan's aggression, but was concerned about the security of the British colonies in Asia. In September 1941, Britain sent a request to Canada for two battalions to help reinforce the colony of Hong Kong.

Britain's Situation in Europe

In the fall of 1941, Britain was facing a serious threat to her national security. She stood alone in Europe, facing a powerful German war machine. From 1936, when Germany entered the Rhineland, German aggression towards its European neighbours went virtually unchecked. Germany annexed Austria in 1938, and invaded Poland the next year. The spring of 1940 saw the German Blitzkrieg attack sweep through Norway, Denmark, the Netherlands, Belgium, and France.

German expansion in Europe, 1937–42.

SERGEANT GANDER

The British Expeditionary Force (BEF), which had been stationed in France, was pushed back against the sea, and only the miraculous evacuation at the Dunkirk beaches[17] saved the BEF from complete annihilation. Although a large number of soldiers were saved all of the British Army's heavy equipment and machinery (guns, trucks, ammunition, and fuel supplies) had to be left behind. Following the Dunkirk evacuation, Britain needed months to re-equip and re-supply its armed forces properly. The critical shortage of materials left the island extremely vulnerable to attack.

The Royal Navy was also stretched beyond its capabilities, having to provide not only homeland defence but also to defend the convoys of war supplies that Britain was importing across the Atlantic to sustain the war effort. They were also providing support for the ground troops in the Mediterranean area and North Africa. The Royal Air Force was busy defending Britain's skies against the waves of punishing German bombers who appeared over the island. It was amidst these circumstances that Britain launched its appeal to Canada for help in reinforcing their Hong Kong garrison.

present" were labeled Class C.[8] Both the Royal Rifles and the Winnipeg Grenadiers were Class C units. General Henry Duncan Graham Crerar,[9] who selected the two units, explained his choice stating, "In order to adhere to the principle of territorial representation, I consider it most desirable that one unit should come from Western Canada and the other from Eastern Canada" and "in the case of the Royal Rifles, there is also the fact that this battalion, while nominally English-speaking, is actually drawn from a region overwhelmingly French-speaking in character and contains an important proportion of Canadians of French-descent."[10] Further, the Hong Kong posting was considered garrison duty and both the Royal Rifles and Winnipeg Grenadiers had experience with that type of assignment.

On October 11, 1941, Colonel J.K. Lawson, the army's director of military training, was promoted to the rank of Brigadier and given command of the two Canadian battalions, nicknamed "C" Force, who had been selected to reinforce Hong Kong.

3: Mascot on the Move

The Royal Rifles were determined not to leave Gander behind. As Rifleman Phil Doddrige remembers, "… he was a favourite of all the men … He was looked after by his handler, Fred Kelly, but I think he had love enough to go around as he showed great affection for all of us. As Regimental Mascot he went everywhere with us, including Hong Kong."[1] Gander travelled with the men to Valcartier Camp (north of Quebec) where the Rifles were given "embarkation leaves," which

Royal Rifles en route to Vancouver (at Valcartier), October 23, 1941.

Courtesy of the National Archives of Canada PA-116794.

Courtesy of the National Archives of Canada PA-126877.

Gander marching with Fred Kelly in Quebec City, 1941.

allowed them to make a final visit home or to enjoy one final holiday, and new light-weight tropical uniforms. Sergeant George MacDonell remembers, "… excitement was high and we were so glad to be leaving our boring garrison duties behind for our new adventure."[2] Some of the men figured that the tropical uniforms meant they were headed to North Africa to serve with the British fighting there.

After the leaves were over and the necessary equipment had been distributed, the Royal Rifles travelled to Quebec City. Gander marched with the troops on parade up to the Plains of Abraham. Once at the top, Fred Kelly found a washroom with shower facilities and treated Gander to a cooling shower before the long, hot descent. The crowds loved him.

Boarding a train in Quebec City, the Rifles were surprised to find themselves heading west towards Vancouver, instead of east towards Halifax (the most likely departure point for the suspected posting to North Africa).[3] On their way westward the train stopped at Winnipeg and the Rifles were joined by the Winnipeg Grenadiers. The combined force of just over two thousand men (and Gander), nicknamed "C" Force and under the command of Brigadier General J.K. Lawson, set off for Vancouver.

Once in Vancouver, however, the Royal Rifles ran into some difficulties with Gander. Fred Kelly was assigned to embark on the HMCS *Prince Robert*, the escort for the troop ship the TSS *Awatea*. The captain of the vessel refused to allow Gander entry, insisting there was no place for a "bear" on his ship. The enlisted men of the Royal Rifles were furious, especially since an officer in their regiment had been allowed to board with his small, black dog. After a tense conference, where the soldiers managed to convince the captain that Gander was, in fact, simply a very *large* dog, Gander was allowed to walk down the gang plank and join his comrades.

It was a difficult start to a voyage that was only going to get worse. The *Awatea,* escorted by the HMCS *Prince Robert*, set sail for Hong Kong, carrying a personnel strength of 1,975. Included were: ninety-six officers, 1,877 other ranks, two civilian auxiliary services supervisors, two nursing sisters, two medical officers, two officers of the Canadian Dental Corps and their assistants, three chaplains, and a detachment of the Canadian Postal Corps.[4] The ships were dreadfully overcrowded. Rifleman Sydney Skelton recalls:

> We walked around on the deck and nearly everywhere was Out of Bounds, No Smoking Below Decks, and only smoking in rooms — officers had the smoking rooms, indeed the officers had everything … Things began to look bad. Supper … came and the lads waited hours for it and it turned out to be tripe and onions, and it really was tripe. One thing led to another and the troops were going to march off the boat … Fifty men got off, and the first time arguing

Gander and the Royal Rifles aboard the HMCS *Prince Robert*, November 15, 1941. Gander is front.

Courtesy of the National Archives of Canada PA-166999.

The *Awatea* and the *Prince Robert*

The Awatea *was built in 1936, and was designed to accommodate 540 passengers, a crew of 342, and weighed in at over 13,000 tons. She travelled at about twenty-three knots, making her one of the fastest liners in the world at that time. The* Awatea *was a New Zealand ship and had made most of its early runs between Auckland and Tasmania, Auckland and Sydney, and from Sydney to Wellington. When the Second World War broke out, she was fitted with a four-inch gun and was used for the transportation of troops and refugees, those civilians arriving from the Philippines and Singapore after the Japanese attacked. She was requisitioned by the British Government in September 1941, to act as a troop transport, and she sailed to Vancouver. Most of the Royal Rifles and Winnipeg Grenadiers travelled to Hong Kong aboard the* Awatea. *Later in the war she was used as a troop ship for the Allied landings in North Africa. On November 8, 1942, the* Awatea *carried troops to Algiers. As she was leaving she was attacked by Italian bombers and sunk.*

The HMCS Prince Robert *was one of three identical "Prince" ships (*Prince Robert, Prince Henry, *and* Prince David*) that the Canadian National Railway ordered built in the 1920s. The* Prince Robert *was launched in 1930, and could accommodate 438 passengers and travel at twenty-two knots. She was used mainly as a cruise ship through the 1930s and when war broke out in 1939 she was requisitioned by the British Admiralty. The* Prince Robert *performed a wide variety of duties for a number of different countries during the Second World War.*

In early 1941 she was attached to New Zealand, to provide convoy protection for airmen coming to Canada for pilot training. By the fall of that year she was requisitioned to act as an escort for the Awatea, *and assist in transporting the Winnipeg Grenadiers and the Royal Rifles to Hong Kong. From 1942–43 the* Prince Robert patrolled the Pacific Ocean, intercepting enemy merchant shipping. In 1943, *she was converted into an auxiliary anti-aircraft cruiser and used to escort convoys in the Mediterranean and was even used by the Americans for operations in the Aleutians, a chain of volcanic islands in the northern Pacific Ocean. In July 1945, she joined the British Fleet and returned to Hong Kong in August to assist in transporting the released Canadian prisoners of war back to Canada. After her distinguished wartime career, the* Prince Robert *was sold back into mercantile service. She was subsequently renamed the* Charlton Sovereign *and later the* Luciana, *and was broken up in 1962.*

was all the result they got. The third time the gangplank was raised and there was nearly a riot. The officers had everything and the rest nothing, so you could hardly blame them.[5]

Gander, however, took it all in stride.

A view of the eastern end of Hong Kong, as seen from the Prince Robert, November 19, 1941.

Courtesy of the National Archives of Canada PA-116457.

"C" Force's staff officers aboard the *Awatea* (l to r): Major C.A. Lyndon, Brigadier J.K. Lawson, Colonel P. Hennessy, and Captain H.S.A. Bush.

The troops were not idle during their voyage east — training was carried out as often as possible. Rifleman Sydney Skelton recorded in his diary that "we have been drilling every day, Bren guns, two-inch mortars, and anti-tank rifles. They keep us busy with that plus drill, fatigue duty etc."[6] There were also lectures about the type of enemy that the Canadians could expect to encounter. Rifleman Ken Cambon remembers being told that "the Japanese were all myopic dwarves who wore thick-rimmed glasses and shrank from close combat. They were notoriously poor at night fighting and would not be able to stand up to the bigger white soldiers who had better weapons. Their pilots were sloppy and cowardly. Their obsolete planes, made of wood, would be easy targets."[7] Such stories reflected the racist nature of the European and Canadian commanders' view of the Japanese, and also served as wartime propoganda to bolster the morale of the soldiers. Similar proganda was practised on both sides.

However, Rifleman Sydney Skelton recalls a different description of what Canadians could expect, from a lecture given to the troops by Major C.A. Lyndon. "He told us to expect almost anything at any time, and he told us if we landed we might have to go right into action. Also he told us we might have the chance of being the first Canadians to go into action in this war. The talk gave us a very grim picture. We were told everything hard about the place and never once did they emphasize anything pleasing. This is no pleasure cruise. It might be another Dunkirk."[8]

After a refuelling stop in Honolulu, where the Canadians had the opportunity to view the doomed American battleships lined up at Pearl Harbor, they continued on to Manila in the Philippines. There, the Canadians picked up an additional escort, the British cruiser the HMS *Danae*. The *Danae* was provided as a result of a message received from the Admiralty that stated, "In view of altered circumstances request you will provide cruiser escort for the *Awatea* from Manila to Hong Kong."[9] Although the "altered circumstances" weren't made clear, there was clearly some feeling that heightened security was required to ensure the Canadian contingent reached their destination. After three weeks at sea, "C" Force arrived in Hong Kong.

4: The Calm Before the Storm

The colony of Hong Kong consisted of a group of islands (the most important of which is called Hong Kong) located just south of the Chinese mainland, the Kowloon Peninsula (ceded by China to the British in 1860), and the New Territories (leased by the British from China in 1898, for niniety-nine years) on the adjoining mainland. Altogether the colony covered an area of about 1,095 square kilometres.[1] The Island of Hong Kong, ceded to the British in 1841, covers an area of about eighty square kilometres, its landscape dominated by mountains with very little flat land to be found. Lying just south of the Tropic of Cancer, Hong Kong has a subtropical climate with hot, humid summers and cooler winters. Strategically located between the Taiwan Strait, the South China Sea, and the Pacific Ocean, it provided an excellent channel for sea traffic between Asia and the rest of the world. Moreover, the deep waters surrounding Hong Kong and its wide, mountain protected harbours combined to make its ports, especially Victoria Harbour, extremely desirable.

Under British rule since the mid-1800s, the colony had a largely Chinese population under the control of a British governor. The population in 1941 was approximately 1,729,000, with about 800,000 of that number living on Hong Kong Island. The Royal Navy had used Hong Kong as its major outpost in Asia up until the end of the First World War, but its position was considered vulnerable. A 1921 War Office Study reported that "there was no chance of making Hong Kong sufficiently secure against attack."[2] It was simply too remote from the nearest sources of any British reinforcements, and its harbours, while ideal for commercial trade, were not large enough to house a fleet of modern ships.[3] Therefore, Britain turned to Singapore and constructed an impressive naval base there, which eventually replaced Hong Kong in terms of naval importance. However, the British still maintained a presence in Hong Kong, and despite the gloomy predictions of

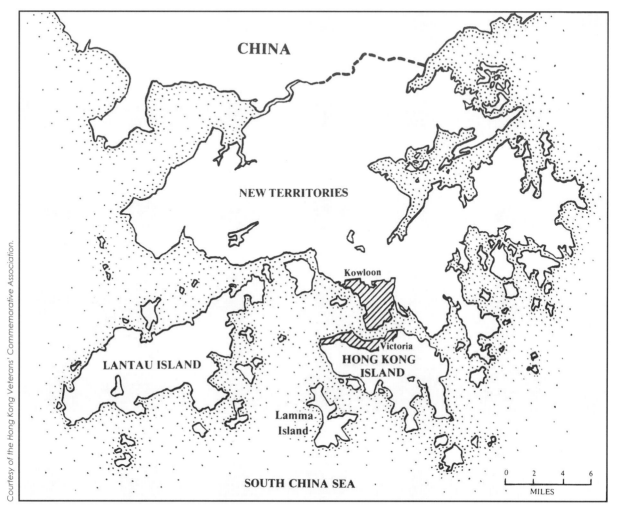

CHINA

NEW TERRITORIES

Kowloon

Victoria
HONG KONG
ISLAND

LANTAU ISLAND

Lamma
Island

SOUTH CHINA SEA

0   2   4   6
MILES

Courtesy of the Hong Kong Veterans' Commemorative Association.

the 1921 report, the 1936 Hong Kong defence scheme stated, "Hong Kong is …
a strategic point vital to the conduct of our Fleet, Army and Air Force."[4]

The Canadians arrived in Hong Kong on November 16, 1941. The soldiers
disembarked and began marching towards Sham Shui Po Barracks, with Gander
leading the way. Rifleman Bruce Cadoret remembers the scene, recalling, "We

The Crown
Colony of Hong
Kong, 1941.

The Royal Rifle's "C" Company infantrymen preparing to disembark from the *Prince Robert*, November 16, 1941.

had our mascot ... our big, black dog leading the march. He walked right up the street there, as proud as could be."[5]

Rifleman Ken Cambon remembers a similarly grand reception, "Our two battalions marched down Nathan Road steel-helmeted and obviously invincible. The main street of Kowloon was lined by cheering crowds waving small Union Jacks."[6] The sight of the jaunty Canadians led by their canine mascot seemed to give a sense of security and hope to a population who had been anxiously watching their borders, ever fearful of Japanese intentions.

Indeed, one Dutch construction engineer, Jan Henrik, who was in Hong Kong on business, noted, "Somehow, their arrival apparently clinched Hong Kong's

SERGEANT GANDER

complacency. In 1939, nobody had thought Hong Kong could be defended successfully. After the arrival of a few thousand Canadians, everybody felt that the Crown Colony could and would be defended successfully. It was a psychological miracle I am unable to explain."[7]

The arrival of the Canadians brought the number of Hong Kong defenders to over 14,000. However, as that number included nursing sisters, the St. John Ambulance Brigade, and the Hong Kong Mule Corps, a transport unit consisting of three officers, 250 men, and ninety mules, the actual number of infantrymen was about 5,422. The remainder of the force was comprised of the Royal Artillery, the Royal Engineers, Hong Kong Volunteer Defence Corps, and the Royal Navy.[8] Prior to that, the Hong Kong forces, under the command of General C.M.

Royal Rifles disembarking HMCS *Prince Robert*, Hong Kong, November 16, 1941.

Courtesy of the National Archives of Canada PA-037419O

Canadian soldiers training in the hills of Hong Kong just prior to the Japanese invasion, December 1941.

Maltby (although the governor, Mark Young, held the title commander-in-chief, the garrison was commanded by Maltby), consisted of only four Regular Army battalions: 2nd Battalion Royal Scots, 1st Battalion the Middlesex Regiment, 5/7 Rajputs, and the 2/14 Punjabis.[9]

For a while things were peaceful, and the Canadians spent their time familiarizing themselves with the island's terrain and its defences. Rifleman John Beebe explains:

SERGEANT GANDER

We lost no time in getting down to work, taking up our posts on guard duty at the permanent dugouts and shelters. These were our future battle stations and we got familiar with the lay of the land during our three day sessions on guard duty. In the following two weeks we got to know the place even better and to like it very well. We drilled hard every morning for two or three hours. We had our own rifles and Brens and although our heavy equipment never arrived, there was plenty of British heavy equipment and we were well trained in its use.[10]

Gander also familiarized himself with the terrain as he accompanied his fellow soldiers on patrol each day. Alongside Fred Kelly, Gander would perform guard duty, occasionally sneaking off for a nap in the shade. During the evenings, in an effort to escape the heat, Gander would sleep in the pillboxes with the men.

The Hong Kong garrison was supported by a much reduced Royal Navy and Royal Air Force presence. The Navy had only one destroyer, eight motor torpedo boats, four river gunboats, a couple of minelayers, and some auxiliary patrol vessels on hand. The air force had only three Vickers Vildebeestes (torpedo bombers) and two Supermarine Walrus amphibians at Kai Tek Airport. Eighteen fixed coastal guns, pill boxes (defensive bun-

Canadian Bren-gun team on a training exercise in the Hong Kong hills prior to the Japanese invasion, December 1941.

kers from which soldiers can defend against enemy attack), minefields, and barbed wire entanglements ringed the island, all put in place to deter an enemy attack. The southern part of the island was the heaviest fortified in expectation of an attack from the sea. The north side of the island, facing the mainland, and Lye Mun Passage (which is only about 412 metres across at its narrowest point) were less fortified.

The precarious state of the island's defensive strength was not lost on Winnipeg Grenadier Private Wilf Lynch, who claimed:

An Indian gun crew manning one of Hong Kong's 9.2 inch coastal defence guns just prior to the Japanese invasion.

SERGEANT GANDER

The minute I got off the boat in Hong Kong, I realized that if the Japanese attacked, they'd wipe us out. We've got no air force, no navy, no place to go, I told my pals. The Japs can back us up to the sea and even the best goddamned swimmer in the Grenadiers couldn't make it all the way back home to Canada.[11]

Despite concerns about the colony's defences, the first several weeks in Hong Kong proved to be quite satisfactory for the Canadians. The Sham Shui Po Barracks, located on the northwest side of Kowloon, were hospitable. Company Quarter Master Sergeant M.S. Standish wrote in a letter home, dated November 20, 1941:

> … you can't imagine the barracks … they are simply beautiful … all made of cement with gardens and grass … you can eat off the sidewalks. I have a hut of my own to sleep in and cook in, and a Chinese boy to look after me. He shines my boots, makes my bed and generally makes himself useful, all for two dollars a week … he's a millionaire at two dollars a week! A man works here at 20 cents a day Hong Kong money and that in Canadian money is less than 6 cents.[12]

As noted earlier, European and Canadian attitudes towards Hong Kong's native Chinese population and the Japanese enemy contained decidedly racist overtones. In wartime it was common practice to actively use negative stereotyping against the enemy to bolster morale among the soldiers who were likely to come face to face with them in combat. They viewed the Japanese as inferior soldiers, a perception that seemingly was largely due to the shape of their eyes. The Allied soldiers were told by their commanders that the Japanese had poor eyesight, and that due to their optical weakness they were not able to fight at night, could not shoot weapons accurately, and that their pilots would not be able to drop their bombs on target.[13]

The Chinese civilians, who made up the majority of Hong Kong's population, fared little better in the eyes of Hong Kong's defensive forces. A British officer told Winnipeg Grenadier Ike Friesen a joke[13] that was making the rounds that clearly demonstrated the use of overt racist propanganda to diminish the value of the Chinese people as human beings.

Gander soon developed his own negative attitude towards the Chinese. According to a story told by Sergeant George MacDonell, the day that the Royal Rifles arrived at Sham Shui Po Barracks "some Chinese tried to lure Gander to the fence, planning to have him for dinner, but Gander escaped after a struggle. After that, Gander lost his faith in the Chinese and would lie in ambush for them when they entered the barracks on business, to the extent that he had to be tied up in the guardroom."[14] The Canadian soldiers encouraged Gander's dislike of Asian people. The Chinese civilians that the soldiers saw on a daily basis were the unfortunate targets of this effort. The local people were leery about passing Gander on the road when he did guard duty. Having never seen the massive Newfoundland breed of dog before, they probably found Gander a strange and scary sight! Fred Kelly would watch as the Chinese would attempt to go around the patrol and then would say, "Gander, go and get them."[15] Gander would charge at them, never biting them, but intimidating them by circling and growling. This unfortunate victimization of the Chinese people may explain, in part, Gander's ferocious response to the Japanese.

By the fall of 1941, the Japanese looked as though they were preparing to move against Hong Kong. In late October they landed 20,000 extra troops in South China, and a Japanese transport stopped in Hong Kong waters was found to have a Japanese general and his staff on board. There was also a report of the Japanese having established a lookout station on one of the small islands off the coast of Hong Kong. On the morning of December 7, 1941, a Punjabi border patrol reported Japanese troop movements of over 20,000 soldiers. Maltby was concerned enough to put the entire Hong Kong garrison on alert.[16]

General Maltby's plan for the defence of Hong Kong entailed dividing his forces into an Island Brigade and a Mainland Brigade. Brigadier Cedric Wallis

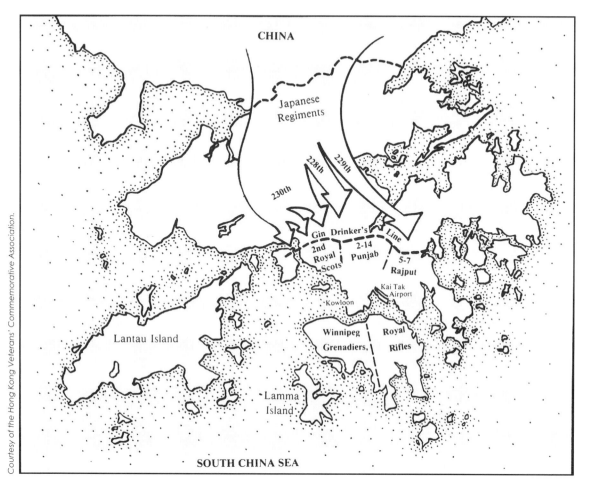

was put in charge of the Mainland Brigade responsible for the mainland section of the colony, including the Kowloon Penninsula and the New Territories. His force consisted of the 2nd Royal Scots, the 2/14 Punjabs, and the 5/7 Rajputs. They were each assigned equal portions of the Gin Drinker's Line, named after nearby Gin Drinkers Bay. This Line was a series of entrenchments protected by barbed wire, with concrete pillboxes reinforcing the line at various strategic points for defence. One of the Punjab companies was positioned for fighting

The initial disposition of forces, December 8, 1941.

THE CALM BEFORE THE STORM

forward of the Line, in the New Territories; their job was to delay attackers and complete demolition assignments before falling back to the Line. If the Gin Drinker's Line was compromised the troops were to render the dockyard and fuel supplies useless to the enemy by blowing them up. Then they were to pull back to the Devil's Peak, a mountain on the Kowloon Peninsula that was garrisoned by the British, enabling them to control the water passage between the mainland part of the colony, the New Territories and Kowloon, and Hong Kong Island. Once there, the troops were to await evacuation across the Lye Mun Passage to Hong Kong Island.

Meanwhile, the Island Brigade, commanded by Canadian Brigadier Lawson, consisted of the two Canadian battalions and the 1st Middlesex. The 1st Middlesex was a machine-gun battalion from Great Britain that was deployed around the island to man pillboxes, fortified defensive bunkers, and other stationary defences, while the Canadians were assigned positions on the coast, to defend against the expected attack from the South China Sea. The Winnipeg Grenadiers operated on the west side of the island, while the Royal Rifles were on the east. Concerns about this deployment of the Canadian forces can be seen in the December 8 entry in the Regimental War Diary,[17] which states:

> The defences on the Island were primarily constructed in anticipation of an attack taking place on Hong Kong from the direction of the sea, while paradoxically all tactical exercises, maneuvers, etc., were always carried out in anticipation of a Japanese attack across the border of the New Territories and moving southwards to Kowloon and Hong Kong.[18]

After the orders were received to activate the entire garrison, the Royal Rifles proceeded to take up their positions on Hong Kong Island. By 1400 hours (2:00 p.m.) most of the Royal Rifles had been ferried across the Lye Mun Passage separating Hong Kong Island from the mainland, and had dispersed to their positions along the fifteen-mile front across the eastern section of the Island.[19]

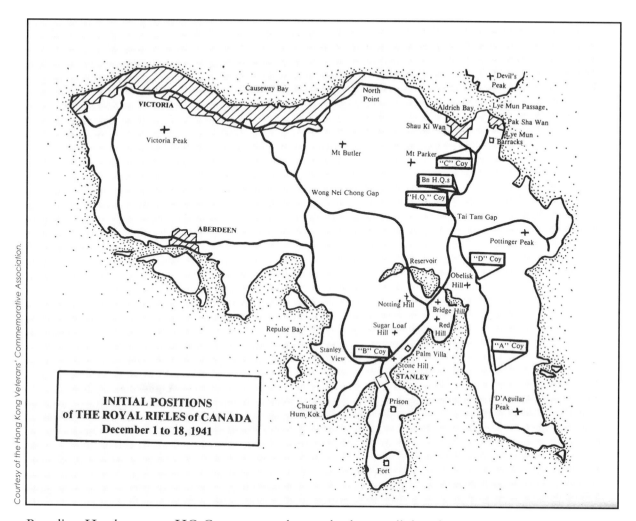

**INITIAL POSITIONS
of THE ROYAL RIFLES of CANADA
December 1 to 18, 1941**

Battalion Headquarters, HQ Company, and several other small detachments were deployed in the Tai Tam area; "A" Company Headquarters and two platoons were at Windy Gap with one platoon at D'Aguilar Point. "B" Company Headquarters and one platoon were at Stanley View, one platoon was between Mary Knowl Convent and Stanley Bay, while a third platoon took up position at the Y in the road leading to Stanley Village.

The initial positions of the Royal Rifles of Canada, December 1 to 18, 1941.

Sergeant Gander's "C" Company was held in reserve in the Lye Mun region with three company platoons and four reinforcement platoons. "D" Company Headquarters was positioned at Obelisk Hill with three platoons at Ty Tam Tuk.[20] Several small detachments of the Hong Kong Volunteer Defence Corps, the Royal Scots, the Middlesex Regiments, and the Rajputs and Punjabs were scattered throughout the positions held by the Royal Rifles.[21] Having taken up their defensive positions the British and Canadian troops could only watch and wait for the inevitable arrival of the Japanese.

5: The Battle Rages

On December 8, 1941, just after the Japanese attack on Pearl Harbor,[1] the Battle of Hong Kong began. At 4:45 a.m. a British intelligence officer monitoring Japanese radio newscasts heard the following message, "The Army and Navy divisions of Imperial Headquarters jointly announced at six o'clock this morning (Tokyo time), December 8, that the Imperial Japanese Army and Navy forces have begun hostilities against the American and British forces in the Pacific at dawn today."[2] However, breakdowns in communications meant that not all units were aware of the outbreak of hostilities. An inefficient telephone system, and the fact that the declaration of hostilities was received over the radio at 4:45 a.m. when many in Hong Kong were still asleep, created this dilemma. Unaware of any declaration of war, the administrative personnel of the Royal Rifles, who were still stationed at Sham Shui Po Barracks, were startled by the appearance of planes overhead. Captain E.L. Hurd recorded the scene in his diary:

> On the morning of December 8th, strange aircraft were noted flying over our Barracks, and a few minutes later three planes returned. At the same time the Air Raid Signal was heard over Kowloon. This was 0800 hrs. and at the time we had received no news about hostilities. I was discussing the alarm with Capt. Thompson, and at the same time noticed three bombs drop from one plane … We dashed into Capt. Barnett's room, just as the bombs hit. Some hit in the Jubillee Bld'g near where our officers were quartered. Another hit still closer, probably forty feet from where we were taking cover. Two others hit in front of the Ration Stores near the main gate. There were several casualties in this area but with the exception of two O.R. of Brigade Staff, they were all

Chinese servants … Fortunately there were no injuries received here on Royal Rifles.[3]

The Japanese bombers released much of their bomb load over Kai Tac Airport, located on the north side of Kowloon Bay, Kowloon, Hong Kong, rendering the facility useless. In one fell swoop the Japanese had achieved air superiority. The pitifully inadequate Royal Air Force stationed there was completely destroyed on the ground, and the nearest RAF station was located over 2,400 kilometres away, in Malaya.[4] On a second pass over Kowloon, the Japanese bombers dropped leaflets demanding the immediate surrender of Hong Kong.

With the achievement of air superiority, the Japanese ground troops marched into the New Territories, the northern most region of the Hong Kong colony, virtually unopposed. As they had been ordered to do by Brigadier Wallis, the forward-based Punjabi contingent commenced the demolition of bridges, roads, and railways, and began their withdrawal towards the Gin Drinker's Line. However, their demolition efforts did little to slow the Japanese movement towards the Island, and by the morning of December 9, their troops were facing the Gin Drinker's Line. By December 10, the Line had been totally penetrated and the British troops were pulling back towards Hong Kong Island. Efforts to slow the Japanese advance were ineffective and General Maltby ordered a general withdrawal. By the morning of December 13, all British and Canadian forces on the mainland had been evacuated to Hong Kong Island.

The Japanese followed up this withdrawal with a request for surrender. It was refused by the British Governor Mark Young, and the Japanese began heavy shelling and bombing of the Island's coastal defences. There were power failures and communications disruptions all over the island, and hundreds of Japanese infiltrators slipped onto the island, creating a pipeline of information to the Japanese commanders about British and Canadian troop movements, ammo dumps, supply depots, pillbox positions, and gun placements.

Sergeant Gander and "C" Company were deployed at Lye Mun. Located a mere 412 metres from the mainland, Lye Mun was an obvious potential crossing point for the Japanese. From December 10–17, the Japanese bombardment of this area was extremely heavy and "C" Company sustained some casualties. The shelling repeatedly knocked out water, electric power, and telephone lines. Organized feeding of the soldiers became almost impossible, since any concentration of men around the kitchen facilities resulted in "heavy and accurate enemy shelling."[5] The men of "C" Company were also "becoming more reluctant to use the telephone system to announce any proposed movement of men as it inevitably resulted in accurate shelling of the route. The lines were obviously tapped by enemy agents."[6]

Gander couldn't stand the noise and frequently took refuge in the pillboxes, although he did accompany the men on their patrols for snipers. The incessant shelling and lack of hot meals took its toll on "C" Company. "They had been unable to rest either by day or by night" and Major Bishop, commander of the Company, requested that they be taken out of the area, for a period of rest.[7] The request for relief was granted, but unfortunately for "C" Company the Japanese invaded before replacements arrived.

A second Japanese request for surrender was submitted on December 17, and it too was refused in a message that stated: "The Governor and Commander-in-Chief of Hong Kong, declines most absolutely to enter into negotiation for the surrender of Hong Kong, and takes this opportunity of notifying Lieut.-Colonel General Sakai and Vice-Admiral Niimi that he is not prepared to receive any further communications from them on the subject."[8]

In response, General Sakai issued the following order to his staff, "On Thursday night, December 18, Japanese Imperial Forces will land upon the Island of Hong Kong at suitable situations between North Point and Lyemun."[9] Late that evening, the Japanese launched their invasion of Hong Kong, sending assault boats, landing craft, and steamers across the Lye Mun Passage, the narrow channel of water that separated Hong Kong from the mainland. All three regiments of the Japanese 38th Division were committed to the attack.

At Lye Mun, the Rajputs were the first line of defence, with "C" Company of the Royal Rifles situated just behind the eastern shoulder of the beachhead.[10] However, "C" Company recorded that "between 2100 and 2200 hours there was

Lye Mun Battery, showing the Lye Mun Passage where the Japanese crossed. The high point in the centre of the photograph is Devil's Peak.

a continual road race of Indian troops running past without arms in the direction of Tai Tam. No information could be obtained from them, they would only say, 'Japs, thousands of Japs.'"[11] As the Japanese began landing on the Canadian-held section of beach, the Royal Rifles laid down heavy gunfire in an effort to slow the approach of the invading forces.

"Now we got our first clear look at the enemy," Rifleman Sydney Skelton remembers:

Swarms of small, shrieking men in khaki jackets, breaches and puttees, helmets bearing the single star, long bayonets, automatic

SERGEANT GANDER

Lye Mun Barracks, the most northern point held by "C" Company.

weapons. They poured out of the landing barges. Some of them threw themselves on the barbed wire while the others streamed over the human bridges. We were on the high ground and we really peppered them. My Bren was hot. But they kept coming. I thought, '… there's no end to them.' Then the planes came in, strafing and bombing, and we fell back.[12]

Gander joined his comrades in the fight, relying on his own best weapons: his size and a strong set of teeth. Despite the ferocity of the fire fight surrounding him, Gander charged at the invaders, running this way and that, snarling and rearing up on his hind legs. Rifleman Reginald Law recalls, "Gander appeared to hate the Japanese on sight. He growled and ran at the enemy soldiers, biting at their heels. And what amazed us all was that they did not shoot him then and there."[13]

By 0100 hours on December 19, it was clear that "C" Company was in danger of being encircled by the Japanese, and the order was given for them to retire southwards. Casualties were high and the evacuation of the wounded slowed the retreat. An excerpt from the "C" Company War Diary describes the condition of the retreating men:

> None … had had a hot meal for five days owing to the destruction of the cooking arrangements. They had been doing continuous manning for over a week with no chance to sleep but in weapon pits. Some would fall down in the roadway and go to sleep … it took several shakings to get them going again.[14]

"C" Company found themselves being pushed back, down Lye Mun Road into the Tai Tam Gap, and later that day into the Stanley area. Gander had continued to challenge the Japanese invaders, who were relentless in their pursuit of the Canadians. When some Japanese soldiers advanced towards a small group of wounded Canadians, Gander charged at them, barking and growling. The Japanese soldiers changed direction and the wounded Canadians avoided being captured or killed. No one is sure why Gander was able to successfully deter the Japanese, but it is unlikely that any Japanese soldier had ever seen a Newfoundland dog before. Gander was truly an incredible sight, standing over six feet tall on his hind legs. An encounter with Gander was probably quite terrifying for the invading troops. Fred Kelly remembers the Chinese civilians' timid reaction to Gander, stating plainly, "I don't think they [had] ever seen a dog that big."[15]

The battle continued to rage through the early hours of December 19, as the Canadians struggled to cover their withdrawal south through the hills of Hong Kong Island. Bullets and explosions screamed through the air. The men of "C" Company fought hard, inflicting (according to a Japanese officer who was interviewed after the war) "sixty-five percent losses on them."[16] The Japanese would lob hand grenades up the hills towards the Canadians, who would try to take cover, or if they were quick, would grab the grenades and lob them back down the hill at the Japanese. As the Canadians struggled to hold their positions, a group of seven wounded Canadians lay along the roadside, pinned down by enemy fire. Suddenly, a Japanese grenade appeared, lofting through the air and coming to rest near the Canadian men.

Hissing and smoking, this grenade spelled death for these Royal Rifles. Staring in horror at the deadly object, the Canadians were distracted when a sudden flash of black streaked past them. Their mascot Gander shot forward, grabbed the grenade in his mouth, and took off running. As Lieutenant Bill Bradley recalls:

> I saw a small group of Japanese soldiers running from something on the road where Captain Gavey and his men were lying badly wounded. One of the men told me later that the soldiers were running from a big dog. They told how Gander had charged out and gathered the grenade in his mouth before it reached the Captain's group.[17]

The grenade exploded in Gander's mouth. Rifleman Reginald Law remembers:

> The last time I saw Gander alive he was running down the road towards the Japanese soldiers. Then there was an overly heavy amount of fire and I heard several grenades exploding close to our group. When the firing eased up I saw Gander lying dead on the road. He was in the open ground, between us and the Japanese, so no one could get close. With the enemy still advancing we had no choice but to leave him.[18]

Gander had given his life to save seven wounded Canadian soldiers. Fred Kelly was devastated to learn of Gander's death. Although the dog was adored by all of the men of the Royal Rifles, Kelly was the one with the closest bond to Gander.

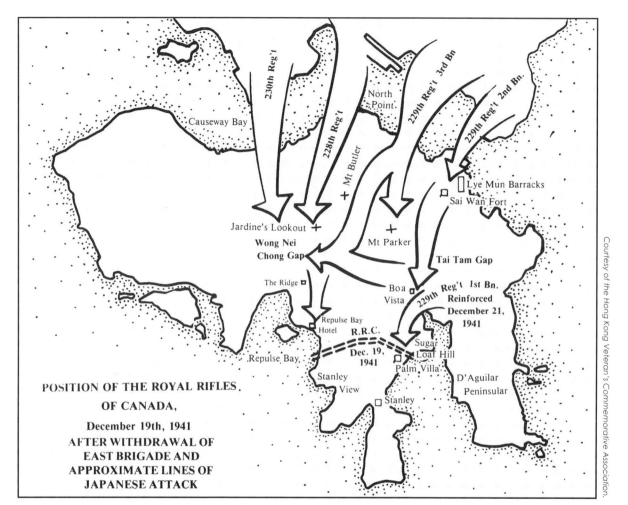

Courtesy of the Hong Kong Veteran's Commemorative Association.

POSITION OF THE ROYAL RIFLES
OF CANADA,
December 19th, 1941
AFTER WITHDRAWAL OF
EAST BRIGADE AND
APPROXIMATE LINES OF
JAPANESE ATTACK

The positions of the Royal Rifles of Canada and the Japanese lines of attack, December 19, 1941.

Kelly remembers, "I seen him the next morning … he was dead the next morning … but I didn't go near. I was so distraught … I didn't go look at him, I just seen him in the distance."[19]

Sergeant Gander's death is recorded in the list of "C" Force Soldiers Killed or Missing in Action or Died of Wounds as occurring December 19, 1941. To be more accurate, his heroic act most likely took place sometime during the night of December 18/19. The confusion of battle makes it difficult to pinpoint events exactly, but it is possible to gauge with some accuracy when his fateful charge took place. It is documented that Lieutenant Bradley, who witnessed the Japanese running down the road away from the injured Captain Gavey (and his men), was ordered, along with Captain Gavey, to attack Sai Wan Fort at 2235 hours on the 18th. Obviously Gavey was not injured at this point, but did sustain his injuries while the Canadians were attempting to disengage after the abortive attack on the Fort, a walled fortification located on Sai Wan Hill. Tony Banham's book, *Not the Slightest Chance*, records the death of Rifleman Gordon Irvine, on December 18, and indicates that Irvine was "killed by the same shell that injured Captain Gavey."[20] This is most likely the injury that left Gavey and his men lying wounded by the side of the road, sometime after 2235 hours on the 18th.

Fred Kelly, who was busy fighting off the Japanese invaders, has indicated that, "The night they landed I took it for granted that Gander was in the pillbox … when they started mortaring and shelling I think what actually happened was he got scared and run out of the pillbox … probably that's when he met the Japanese."[21] Kelly confirms that Gander was killed the first night the Japanese landed on Hong Kong and that he didn't actually see what happened to Gander because "it was pitch dark."[22] Kelly also indicates that he saw Gander's body the next morning. Clearly, sometime during the late hours of December 18 or the early hours of December 19, Gander's war came to an end.

Despite the loss of their mascot the Royal Rifles had to continue the fight. It was a lost cause, however. The Japanese continued to press their advance, and although several brave counter attacks were made by the British and Canadians across the Island, they were outnumbered and outgunned. A soldier from the Royal Rifles recalls:

> Christmas night, we were up on a ridge in front of Fort Stanley waiting for an attack. There was no attack because there was a truce at the time, pending negotiations between the governor of the Island and the invading forces. The most frightening thing

POW information

There are countless eyewitness reports of the brutality towards civilians and captured soldiers that was demonstrated by the Japanese. Many of these atrocities were addressed at the Hong Kong War Crimes court in 1946. The Japanese's brutal treatment of their prisoners stemmed largely from the fact that they never ratified the 1929 Geneva Convention,[27] which outlined what was deemed as acceptable conduct regarding the treatment of prisoners of war. Moreover, Japanese soldiers were encouraged to perceive being taken prisoner as shameful, and their soldiers' handbook stated, "Do not fall captive, even if the alternative is death … Bear in mind the fact that to be captured not only means disgracing the army, but your parents and family will never be able to hold up their heads again. Always save the last round for yourself."[28]

With this type of mindset it's hardly surprising that the Canadian prisoners of war were treated so badly. After their surrender the Royal Rifles were transported across Hong Kong Island to the North Point Camp. The Winnipeg Grenadiers were taken back to the mainland and housed at Sham Shui Po until January 23, 1942, when they and the Royal Navy prisoners were taken back to the Island to join the Royal Rifles at the North Point Camp. Three months later the Royal Navy prisoners were moved again and North Point became an all-Canadian camp.[29] In September of 1942, the Canadians were moved back to Sham Shui Po on the mainland, which had been largely vacated due to the transfer of the British prisoners housed there to work camps in Japan. Throughout 1943 and 1944 the Canadians were also transferred to work camps in Japan, where they were forced to work in coal and iron mines, and in the dockyards.

No matter where the prisoners were located, their living conditions and treatment by the Japanese were brutal. Living quarters were always crowded and poor sanitary conditions prevailed. Food was inadequate at best, and there was an acute lack of medical supplies. Diseases such as beri beri, pellagra, dysentery, and diphtheria were prevalent in the camps. The Japanese guards were often ruthless in their treatment of the prisoners and "slaps, blows from fists and rifle butts, or prods from bayonets for the slightest transgression" were not uncommon.[30]

was looking out and seeing the glow of thousands of cigarettes. The Japanese down below had been told we'd surrendered, so they all sat down and started smoking cigarettes. Then we realized how close they were, and how many they were, and how impotent we were.[23]

On Christmas Day the Allied forces on Hong Kong surrendered to the Japanese. At the time of surrender the East Brigade had been pushed down into the tip of the Stanley peninsula, and the West Brigade held a line that ran roughly from Bowrington in the north to Aberdeen in the south — less than a quarter of the Island's territory was held between them.[24]

The Hong Kong garrison reported over 2,000 men killed or missing, with twice that number being wounded. The Canadians incurred 290 fatalities, with nearly 500 wounded.[25] Those who had not been killed in the battle were

Courtesy of the National Archives of Canada PR-483.

Commander Peter MacRitchie of the *Prince Robert* meeting with liberated Canadian POWs at Sham Shui Po Camp, September 1945.

destined to spend the rest of the war living in horrific conditions in Japanese prisoner of war camps. Those who survived the camps returned home to Canada when the Japanese surrendered in 1945, and they never forgot their heroic canine comrade who had made the ultimate sacrifice during the Battle of Hong Kong. Sergeant George MacDonell states, emphatically, "No two-legged soldier did his duty any better and none died more heroically than Sergeant Gander."[26]

The prisoners were liberated in August 1945, when the Japanese surrendered to the Allied forces. At the end of August the transport ships that would carry the surviving Canadians back home to Canada arrived. Ironically, one of these ships was the *Prince Robert*, which had transported many of the Royal Rifles to Hong Kong back in 1941. The number of Canadians who returned home was markedly fewer than had made the journey to Hong Kong. In addition to all of the men lost in the battle, 128 died in the Hong Kong POW camps, 136 died in work camps in Japan, and four men were executed after an escape attempt. In total, 557 of the original Canadian contingent did not return home.[29]

6: Gander Gets His Medal

The Canadian soldiers who returned to Canada formed the Hong Kong Veterans' Association (HKVA) in 1948, in response to a wide variety of complaints that the veterans had experienced since returning home. Many had returned from Hong Kong with a range of medical ailments resulting from their captivity, and they felt that existing government benefits and compensation were inadequate to address their needs. They also wanted compensation for their years of forced labour in Japan's work camps. In 1965, they ratified their association's constitution, which listed the aims of the HKVA as:

> To assist all members in times of need,
> To maintain and improve social welfare and friendship among members and their dependents"
> To promote legislation for the physical well being of all members of "C" force or Allied personnel who were imprisoned by Japan 1941–1945.[1]

As a result of the HKVA's determined advocacy, significant gains were made in terms of compensating the veterans and their families, for their service in Hong Kong.

As health concerns and advancing age began to impact the HKVA's ability to fulfill their association's agenda, a proposal was made in 1993 to create a new association, made up of the sons and daughters of "C" Force veterans. In 1995, the new association was given the name the Hong Kong Veterans' Commemorative Association (HKVCA). Their mission is describd as "to educate all Canadians on the role of Canada's soldiers in the Battle of Hong Kong and on the effects of the internment of the battle's survivors on both the soldiers and their families. We

Company
Sergeant
Major Osborn,
Winnipeg
Grenadiers,
Jamaica,
1940/41.

Sergeant Major John Osborn

John Robert Osborn was born in England in 1899 and saw action in the First World War as a seaman in the Royal Naval Volunteer Reserve. After the war he immigrated to Canada, where he farmed and worked for the Canadian Pacific Railway. He married and had five children. In 1933, he joined the Winnipeg Grenadiers and was called to active duty six years later, in September 1939. Sergeant Major John Osborn was the first Canadian to receive the Victoria Cross in the Second World War, and his was the only Victoria Cross awarded for the Battle of Hong Kong. It is on display at the Canadian War Museum in Ottawa. He was forty-two years old when he died and has no known grave, but his name can be seen on the Hong Kong Memorial at the entrance to the Botanic Gardens in Victoria, Hong Kong.

Sergeant Major John Osborn's Citation

At Hong Kong, on the morning of the 19th of December 1941, a company of the Winnipeg Grenadiers to which Company Sergeant-Major Osborn belonged, became divided during an attack on Mount Butler, a hill rising steeply above sea level. A part of the company led by Company Sergeant-Major Osborn captured the hill at the point of the bayonet and held it for three hours when, owing to the superior numbers of the enemy and to fire from an unprotected flank, the position became untenable. Company Sergeant-Major Osborn and a small group covered the withdrawal, and when their turn came to fall back, Osborn, single-handed, engaged the enemy while the remainder successfully joined the company. Company Sergeant-Major Osborn had to run the gauntlet of heavy rifle and machine-gun fire. With no consideration for his own safety, he assisted and directed stragglers to the new company position, exposing himself to heavy enemy fire to cover their retirement. Wherever danger threatened he was there to encourage his men.

During the afternoon the company was cut off from the battalion and completely surrounded by the enemy, who were able to approach to within grenade throwing distance of the slight depression which the company was holding. Several enemy grenades were thrown, which Sergeant-Major Osborn picked up and threw back. The enemy threw a grenade, which landed in a position where it was impossible to pick it up and return it in time. Shouting a warning to his comrades this gallant Warrant Officer threw himself on the grenade, which exploded, killing him instantly. His self-sacrifice undoubtedly saved the lives of many others.

Company Sergeant-Major Osborn was an inspiring example to all throughout the defence which he assisted so magnificently in maintaining against an overwhelming enemy force for over eight and a half hours, and in his death he displayed the highest quality of heroism and self-sacrifice.

also assist in the support and welfare of Hong Kong veterans and their widows."[2] In 2001, the administration and finances of the two groups were merged. The HKVA still participates in its own in commemorative programs with Veterans' Affairs Canada, and also plays an active role in the HKVCA by educating Canadians about the Battle of Hong Kong.

The men of the Royal Rifles of Canada always felt that Gander deserved recognition for his selfless act. In 1995, Jeremy Swanson, then commemorations officer at the

Canadian War Museum, heard the story of Gander from some of the veterans. The veterans had come together for a special meeting of the HKVA where they all received their Hong Kong clasps, an award introduced by the Canadian government in July 1995 to recognize the contributions made by the Canadian soldiers at the Battle of Hong Kong. They were reminiscing about the story of Sergeant Major J.R. Osborn, the Canadian soldier who had been awarded the Victoria Cross for his heroism at the Battle of Hong Kong. Osborn had saved the lives of several men in his company by throwing himself on top of a Japanese grenade.

As they chatted about the Sergeant Major's heroism one of the veterans made the comment, "Just like that damned dog." Swanson's interest was piqued and he quizzed the veterans for more information. From what Swanson could glean, Gander, the canine mascot of the Royal Rifles of Canada, had performed an act of heroism that was strikingly similar to that of Sergeant Major Osborn's. Fascinated by Gander's story, Swanson and a small group of volunteers, including Howard Stutt of McGill University, began researching the tale to verify its truthfulness and to separate fact from fiction. After researching Gander's story extensively, Swanson

Jeremy Swanson

Jeremy Swanson was the commemorations and operations officer to Programs and Collections at the Canadian War Museum (CWM) from 1992–2002. An emigrant from South Africa, Swanson has played a vital and active role in helping to research and preserve Canadian military history. During his tenure with the CWM, Swanson conducted research and historical overviews of numerous CWM exhibitions and literary projects, including "Canada's Armed Forces 1945–50" and "Canada in Korea," as well as planning and leading a successful search for families of the twenty-six Canadian airmen killed over Poland during the Second World War.

Swanson helped spearhead the campaign for Sergeant Gander's PDSA Dickin Medal, committing hundreds of hours to research, and was responsible for organizing the PDSA Dickin Medal ceremony that was held at the British High Commission in Ottawa in October 2000. Currently, Swanson is working as a men's rights activist in Ottawa.

unearthed numerous military and eyewitness accounts of Gander's heroism. Swanson felt strongly that Gander was deserving of a posthumous award for bravery.

The People's Dispensary for Sick Animals (PDSA) is a veterinary charity in the United Kingdom that was founded in 1917 by Maria Dickin. Born in London in 1870, Dickin (Mia to her friends) was the daughter of a minister and the eldest of eight children. At twenty-eight years of age she married her wealthy cousin, Arnold Dickin, and gave up her job — she owned a successful voice production studio — to look after her new household and assume the role of society wife. Horrified by the plight of the animals in London's poverty-stricken East End, Dickin explained that "the suffering and misery of these poor uncared for creatures was a revelation to me. I had no idea it existed and it made me indescribably miserable."[3]

She decided to make the provision of veterinary care for the poor her social cause, and on November 17, 1917, she opened her first dispensary. A notice advertising the opening read simply: "Bring your sick animals. Do not let them

Victoria Cross

Introduced by Queen Victoria in 1856, to reward acts of valour during the Crimean War (1853–56), the Victoria Cross (VC) is the highest award for valour "in the face of the enemy" in the United Kingdom, some Commonwealth countries, and former British Empire territories. It may be awarded to any enlisted personnel (any rank) or civilians under military command. The VC is awarded for, "most conspicuous bravery, or some daring or pre-eminent act of valour or self sacrifice, or extreme devotion to duty in the presence of the enemy." The medal is extremely rare, having been awarded only 1,356 times to 1,353 recipients since its inception.[6] It is a bronze cross with a Crown and Lion superimposed and the words, "For Valour." Ninety-four Canadians have been awarded the British Victoria Cross, none since 1945. Since Newfoundland was not part of Canada prior to 1945, Victoria Cross recipients from Newfoundland are identified separately. In 1993, it was decided that Canadians would no longer be eligible for the British Victoria Cross — it was replaced by a Canadian Victoria Cross and has yet to be awarded.

Fred Kelly with Rimshot.

suffer. All animals treated. All treatment free."[4] The response was overwhelming, and soon Dickin began opening more dispensaries. By 1935, she had established five PDSA hospitals, seventy-one dispensaries, and eleven mobile dispensaries, eventually expanding her philanthropic endeavours to Greece, Egypt, South Africa, and Palestine. Although Dickin died in 1951, at the age of eighty-one, her legacy to the care of animals continues as the PDSA is still going strong today.

SERGEANT GANDER

Courtesy of the Hong Kong Veterans' Commemorative Association

Maria Dickin established the PDSA Dickin Medal in 1943 to recognize "any animal displaying conspicuous gallantry or devotion to duty whilst serving with the British Commonwealth armed forces or civil emergency services."[5] The bronze medallion bears the words, "For Gallantry" and "We Also Serve" and is considered the animals' Victoria Cross. Since its inception it has been awarded sixty-two times (as of 2008). With the documentation provided by Jeremy Swanson, the Hong Kong Veterans' Association forwarded an application to the PDSA requesting that Gander be considered for the PDSA Dickin Medal.

The PDSA was stunned to receive the medal request, as no such request had been submitted in over fifty years. After reviewing the extensive documentation

Gander's medal ceremony. Jeremy Swanson (far left), Fred Kelly (holding leash), Rimshot (front), and Eileen Elms (nee Chafe, the little girl from the sled photograph).

accompanying the application for Gander's medal the PDSA quickly approved awarding the medal to Gander. Then PDSA Director General Marilyn Rydstrom stated, "We were surprised to receive the Association's request and comprehensive support documentation — the first in over fifty years to be submitted to the PDSA. Gander's story exemplifies the heroism displayed by many animals who served alongside British and Commonwealth forces during the Second World War. In some cases they performed outstanding acts, as did Gander, while others played equally significant roles by boosting morale among prisoners of war, carrying vital messages, and detecting humans and animals buried under bomb damaged buildings. We are delighted to add Gander's name to this illustrious list."[7]

On October 27, 2000, an award ceremony was held at the British High Commission in Ottawa. Members of the PDSA, the Hong Kong Veterans' Association, and the Royal Rifles of Canada, as well as many other invited guests, were on hand as Gander's old handler, Fred Kelly, accepted Gander's medal from PDSA Chairman Sir Roland Guy. Kelly, gently patting Rimshot, the Newfoundland dog that had been brought in to represent Gander, stated, "It's an honour just to be able to put my hand on this dog."[8] Then, with his emotions taking over, Kelly declared, "I only wish that Gander had lived so that I could have taken him home. This is the happiest day of my life."[9]

Jeremy Swanson, who spent over five years researching and documenting Gander's story, was equally pleased, stating, "I feel absolutely overjoyed seeing the joy in the faces of those veterans. For me, it marks the successful end of a project that created a new Canadian hero."[10]

Gander's Citation

For saving the lives of Canadian Infantrymen during the Battle of Lye Mun on Hong Kong Island in December 1941. On three documented occasions "Gander" the Newfoundland mascot of the Royal Rifles of Canada engaged the enemy as his regiment joined the Winnipeg Grenadiers, members of Battalion Headquarters "C" Force and other Commonwealth troops in their courageous defence of the

DEC. 8 - 25 · 1941

GANDER, ONE OF CANAD
'C' FORCE HEROES DURI
THE DEFENCE OF HONG

Pen and ink sketch of Gander.

Island. Twice "Gander's" attacks halted the enemy's advance and protected groups of wounded soldiers. In a final act of bravery the war dog was killed in action gathering a grenade. Without "Gander's" intervention many more lives would have been lost in the assault.

The medal was given to the Canadian War Museum for its exhibit on the Defence of Hong Kong. Sadly, the PDSA's hope that the exhibition of Gander's medal would remind generations to come of Canada's courageous canine has not been realized. The medal was exhibited for a time, but has since been removed. At present, Gander's story is no longer part of the Hong Kong exhibit at the War Museum, and his PDSA Dickin Medal is kept in a secure vault in the basement of the Museum.

7: Animals at War

The history of military conflict abounds with stories and descriptions of how animals served alongside human combatants. Whether as a much loved mascot providing moral support or a link to home, or as a working animal trained to carry messages, sniff out bombs, or charge into battle with a soldier perched upon its back, animals have been as much a part of military history as the battles themselves. The contributions of these creatures, who never had a choice about whether or not they wanted to "go off to war," have been recognized by many of the nations for which they served.

In the Canadian capital of Ottawa, the stone wall at the entrance to the Memorial Chamber in the Parliament buildings has carvings depicting animals and the words, "The Humble Beasts that Served and Died." In Lille, France, a statue of a woman with a pigeon sitting in her hands stands as a memorial to all of the carrier pigeons who transported messages during the wars. Great Britain has perhaps the most impressive memorial, The Animals in War Memorial, which was unveiled in 2004 and is located in Hyde Park. The inscription reads, "Animals in War. This monument is dedicated to all the animals that served and died alongside British and allied forces in wars and campaigns throughout time. They had no choice."

As workers, animals have served a multitude of purposes throughout the history of war. Dogs have routinely been used to search for both mines and injured people, and more recently dolphins and sea lions are being trained to search for underwater mines. Mules, camels, elephants, and oxen have traditionally been used for the transport of supplies, while horses have carried both men and supplies into battle. Over eight million horses were killed during the First World War alone. Pigeons were used extensively to carry messages during both World Wars, and in the Second World War over 200,000 were used, with only one in eight ever returning home.[1] Even glow-worms have served, providing light in the trenches during the First World War so that the soldiers could read.

Courtesy of the PDSA.

British soldiers in line to register their mascots as members of the Allied Forces Mascot Club.

During the First World War one of the most famous working animals was Murphy, the donkey. In 1915, he was shipped to Turkey, where Australian and New Zealand troops were fighting Turkish and German forces at Gallipoli. Along with the other donkeys, Murphy carried supplies up and down the hills adjacent to the beach. One day, an Australian soldier named John Simpson Kirkpatrick (more commonly known as Simpson) saw Murphy carrying his load of supplies

and came up with another idea for the donkey's use. He threw a blanket over Murphy's back to act as a saddle and rode the little donkey through the hills searching for injured soldiers. Simpson would put the injured men on Murphy's back, and Murphy would carry them down to the medical unit. The idea worked well and each day Simpson and Murphy would set off in search of wounded, scouring the hills from dawn until dusk, always under threat of enemy fire. Their hard work resulted in the rescue of over 300 wounded men. On May 19, 1915,

Polish sailors and their ships' cats, 1940.

Convoy the ship's cat of HMS *Hermione*, November 26, 1941.

while on one of their patrols, Simpson and Murphy came under heavy enemy fire, just after they placed a wounded man on the donkey's back. Simpson was killed. Legend has it that Murphy continued back to the army hospital with the injured man on his back and then led rescuers back to Simpson's body. Other sources claim that Murphy was killed in the initial gunfire barrage. Whatever the case, the Australians thought enough of the pair's contributions to erect a statue of Simpson and Murphy outside the Australian War Memorial in Canberra.

Courtesy of the Imperial War Museum A-6411.

SERGEANT GANDER

Courtesy of the Imperial War Museum A-11576.

Humankind's bond with animals fostered the need for many soldiers to bring mascots with them into battle, or to adopt an animal while serving in the military. A pet, something to love and care for, is often a welcome distraction from the horrors of war. During the Second World War the PDSA formed the Allied Forces Mascot Club to recognize the importance of animal mascots and the variety of roles that they played while serving with the armed forces. Hundreds of soldiers and sailors registered their mascots for membership in the club, and each animal

Ship's mascot Ighty who was injured at Dieppe, September 1942.

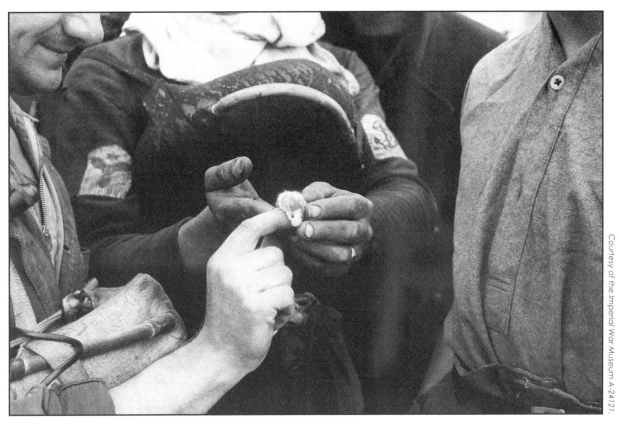

Eustace the mouse, on board *LCT 947*, Normandy, June 6, 1944.

member received a certificate and a badge to recognize their wartime service. The mascots took on all shapes and sizes of many different animals.

In addition to Sergeant Gander, there are two other relatively well-known Canadian animals that set off to war with their masters. The first never actually made it to the battlefields, but is probably the most famous, being better known as the bear that inspired the creation of Winnie the Pooh. In 1914, just after the outbreak of the First World War, a young veterinarian from Winnipeg, Harry Colebourn, set off for the newly created army training camp at Valcartier, Quebec. At a train stop in White River, Ontario, Harry befriended a small black bear cub whose mother had been killed by a trapper. He paid twenty dollars for her and

SERGEANT GANDER

Muncher, the rabbit mascot of the HMCS *Haida*.

Winnie and Harry
Colebourn.

Courtesy of the Provincial Archives of Manitoba, Colebourn, D. Harry Collection, No. N10467.

named her Winnie (after his hometown of Winnipeg). Winnie became the mascot of Colebourn's infantry brigade. She sailed to England with her new friends and ended her journey at England's Salisbury Plains, the principal training ground for British and Commonwealth troops during the war.

Winnie slept in Colebourn's tent (under his cot) and became like a pet to many of the men training there. She would follow them around, playing with them and entertaining them with her antics, and "her presence helped take their minds off their ongoing soggy circumstances and off the prospect of the conflict to come. Group photographs frequently included Winnie, front and centre, a position of honour."[2] Unfortunately (or perhaps, fortunately for Winnie) Winnie's days a mascot were coming to an end. In early December of 1914, Colebourn was given orders that Winnie needed to be removed from Brigade Headquarters as the unit was preparing for departure to France. A bear cub simply could not be accommodated in a war zone. Colebourn made arrangements to "loan" Winnie to the London Zoo. The Canadian bear went on to become one of the Zoo's star attractions, and one of her biggest fans was a young boy named Christopher Robin Milne, whose father was a writer. Christopher Robin named his own teddy bear after Winnie and his father wrote several stories about the boy and his bear. At the end of the war Colebourn officially donated Winnie to the London Zoo, and she lived there until her death in 1934.

Another Canadian animal that actually did experience war belonged to Dr. John McCrae, author of the poem "In Flander's Fields." Shortly before the outbreak of the First World War, McCrae was given a horse as a gift. He took the horse to Europe with him, and frequently travelled by horseback to make his medical rounds and to reach the wounded men on the battlefield. The horse, named Bonfire, earned a special place in McCrae's heart, and McCrae often mentioned Bonfire in his letters home. In one such letter, he wrote, "I have a very deep affection for Bonfire, for we have been through so much together, and some of it bad enough. All the hard spots to which one's memory turns the old fellow has shared, though he says so little about it."[3] One can only imagine the horrors witnessed by both McCrae and Bonfire during McCrae's time as a field surgeon on the front lines.

John McCrae
and Bonfire,
1916.

McCrae would also send letters to his sister's children, written by Bonfire. One, written to his nephew Jack Kilgour, October 1, 1916, reads as follows, "...do you ever eat blackberries. My master and I pick them every day on the hedges. I like twenty at a time. My leg is better but I have a lump on my tummy. I went to see my doctor today and he says it is nothing at all. I have another horse staying in my stable now; he is black and about half my size. He does not keep me awake at night. Yours truly, Bonfire."[4] The letters were always signed with a hand-drawn hoof print. When McCrae died during the final year of the war, Bonfire marched in his funeral procession.

Working animals and mascots have both been involved in heroic acts that

SERGEANT GANDER

have earned them the PDSA Dickin Medal; intended to acknowledge an animal's gallantry and devotion to duty while with the military or civilian defence, it has been awarded sixty-two times as of December 2008. Its recipients have included horses, pigeons, dogs, and a cat.

Other PDSA Dickin Medal Stories

Pigeons have won more PDSA Dickin Medals than any other animal. Their incredible "homing" instinct made them an integral part of military communications. Man-made communication systems, such as telephones and telegraphs, were often difficult to set up in battlefield conditions and were vulnerable to destruction by the enemy, so pigeons were often used to carry messages in tiny canisters attached to their legs. Many fell victim to bad weather, sniper fire, or to hawks and other birds of prey that the enemy would use to attack the pigeon post.

Winkie receiving her PDSA Dickin Medal from Maria Dickin.

Courtesy of the PDSA.

Irma.

Winkie and Mary of Exeter were two pigeons used during the Second World War whose service earned them the PDSA Dickin Medal. Winkie was aboard a badly damaged Royal Air Force plane that was forced to ditch in the North Sea. The plane, riddled with enemy bullets, was returning home from a mission in Norway. The crew was thrown into the water and found themselves clinging to debris. Winkie's broken container had also been thrown from the plane and she freed herself. Her wings were covered in the oil that was leaking from the wreckage, but she managed to take flight and head for home. She returned to her loft the next morning, soaked with both oil and water. A sergeant from the RAF Pigeon Service was able to identify which plane she had been on and to log a route to the plane wreckage, using wind direction, and predicted flight timing from the time the plane ditched and when Winkie returned home. A rescue team located the downed airmen. Just over a year later, Winkie was awarded the PDSA Dickin Medal, "For delivering a message under exceptionally difficult conditions and so contributing to the rescue of an Air Crew while serving with the RAF in February 1942."

Mary of Exeter was another member of the British National Pigeon Service. She served her country for five years and was wounded twenty-two times, most often

SERGEANT GANDER

by enemy birds of prey. After one mission, Mary returned with three bullet wounds and part of her wing shot off. Despite being badly hurt, she still completed her mission to bring her message home.

The only cat ever to be awarded the PDSA Dickin Medal was a black and white tomcat named Simon. Simon joined the crew of the HMS Amethyst *in 1948. On a mission on China's Yangze River, the* Amethyst *came under fire from Communist shore batteries. A direct hit on the ship's captain's cabin badly injured Simon — his whiskers were burned off, his fur was singed, and he sustained several shrapnel wounds. Pinned down on the river by enemy fire, the* Amethyst *was besieged all summer. Rats on board the ship began spoiling food and stealing from the supplies. The men were fearful and depressed. Simon spent his days patrolling the ship, hunting to help control the rat population. In the evenings he visited*

Courtesy of the PDSA.

Simon, playing while in quarantine.

the sick bay, providing comfort and companionship to the injured sailors. In July 1949, after being stranded for three months, the Amethyst *finally broke free from the river. Simon's contribution throughout the ordeal was widely recognized by his ship mates, and his commanding officer recommended him for the PDSA Dickin Medal. Unfortunately, Simon's medal had to be awarded posthumously. During his* six-month quarantine after his arrival in England, Simon became ill and died. His citation reads, "Served on the HMS Amethyst *during the Yangtze Incident, disposing of many rats though wounded by shell blast. Throughout the incident his behaviour was of the highest order.*"

The PDSA Dickin Medal has been awarded to dozens of dogs for a wide variety of heroic acts. During the Second World War thousands of bombs were dropped on the City of London. After each round of bombing, rescuers combed the debris in search of survivors. Dogs, with their keen sense of smell, were an integral part of this rescue effort. Margaret Griffin had two Alsation dogs, Psych and Irma, who were well trained in performing search and rescue missions. Griffin kept extensive and detailed records of her dogs' work throughout the London Blitz. A typical diary entry reads as follows,

> Call to Osborne Road, Tottenham at 21:00 hrs. In house No. 1 Irma found two live casualties. In No. 2 Irma again gave good indication just to one side of [a] fairly large and fierce fire burning through collapsed house debris … Family of five found. In No. 3 a strong indication from Irma over the debris. Rescue found a live cat. Working over No. 4 I got another clear indication under a collapsed floor, later had report from Rescue Leader on this site that 4 adults had been taken, 2 more located and one was suspected lying behind the 2 located ones….[5]

Irma located twenty-one live victims and 170 dead victims, as well as several pets. She was awarded the PDSA Dickin Medal for "being responsible for the rescue of persons trapped under blitzed buildings while serving with the Civil Defence Services in London."

There was also a group known as the Animal Rescue Squad who were determined to help recover any pets that were trapped beneath London's bombed out buildings. One of the group's officers, Bill Barnet, used his terrier Beauty to help locate victims. Beauty eventually rescued over sixty trapped pets, often digging amidst the rubble until her paws were bloody and sore. Beauty's PDSA Dickin Medal was awarded to her for being "the pioneer dog in locating buried air-raid victims while serving with a PDSA rescue squad."

The Ilford PDSA Animal Cemetery is the final resting place of over 3,000 animals, including several of the PDSA Dickin Medal winners. Dating back to the 1920s, the cemetery is located just behind the Ilford PDSA branch. Its design reflects the colours of the PDSA Dickin Medal ribbon — brown, green, and blue, colours that symbolize the land, sea, and air forces. Those interested in paying their respects to animals who served in the war are encouraged to visit this cemetery. A quiet and reflective place, it is a fitting memorial not only to much loved pets, but to those animals who served their country in its darkest hours.

Beauty.

Conclusion

Sergeant Gander was one of hundreds, if not thousands, of animals who acted as a mascot for a military unit during wartime. He provided love and companionship to his fellow soldiers and was a link to home — to a kinder and gentler time when a dog might lie at one's feet in front of a fireplace, with a casual lick to the hand to let its owner know that all was well. In his role as a military mascot, Sergeant Gander was not unique. However, during the bloody night of December 18/19, 1941, he became more than a mascot by consciously, or unconsciously, putting his life on the line to protect a small group of wounded Canadians.

How interesting it is that Gander's heroic act mirrors, almost exactly, the heroism demonstrated by Major John Osborn. Both saw a grenade land, both recognized the danger of the hissing and smoking weapon, and both made a decision to act accordingly. Obviously, Gander may not have had the ability to predict the outcome of his actions, but he took action nonetheless, and that makes him no less a hero than his human counterpart. For his role in saving those Canadian soldiers at the Battle of Hong Kong, and as the only Canadian recipient of the prestigious PDSA Dickin Medal, Sergeant Gander deserves recognition by the Canadian public and the Canadian government. Sergeant Gander has earned his place in history alongside all of the other brave combatants in battle, and his story needs to be told again and again, so that future generations of Canadians may speak his name with pride.

Dogs: Roll of Honour

Bob — Mongrel
6th Royal West Kent Regiment
Date of Award: March 24, 1944
> "For constant devotion to duty with special mention of Patrol work at Green Hill, North Africa, while serving with the 6th Battalion Queens Own Royal West Kent Regt."

Jet — Alsatian
MAP Serving with Civil Defence
Date of Award: January 12, 1945
> "For being responsible for the rescue of persons trapped under blitzed buildings while serving with the Civil Defence Services of London."

Irma — Alsatian
MAP Serving with Civil Defence
Date of Award: January 12, 1945
> "For being responsible for the rescue of persons trapped under blitzed buildings while serving with the Civil Defences of London."

Beauty — Wire-Haired Terrier
PDSA Rescue Squad
Date of Award: January 12, 1945
> "For being the pioneer dog in locating buried air-raid victims while serving with a PDSA Rescue Squad."

Rob — Collie
War Dog No. 471/332 Special Air Service
Date of Award: January 23, 1945
> "Took part in landings during North African Campaign with an Infantry unit and later served with a Special Air Unit in Italy as patrol and guard on small detachments lying-up

Rip, saving a young boy from a bombed-out building in London, England.

in enemy territory. His presence with these parties saved many of them from discovery and subsequent capture or destruction. Rob made over 20 parachute descents."

Thorn — Alsatian
MAP Serving with Civil Defence
Date of Award: March 2, 1945
"For locating air-raid casualties in spite of thick smoke in a burning building."

Rifleman Khan — Alsatian
147 6th Battalion Cameronians (SR)

SERGEANT GANDER

Date of Award: March 27, 1945

> "For rescuing L/Cpl. Muldoon from drowning under heavy shell fire at the assault of Walcheren, November 1944, while serving with the 6th Cameronians (SR)."

Rex — Alsatian
MAP Civil Defence Rescue Dog
Date of Award: April 1945

> "For outstanding good work in the location of casualties in burning buildings. Undaunted by smoldering debris, thick smoke, intense heat and jets of water from fire hoses, this dog displayed uncanny intelligence and outstanding determination in his efforts to follow up any scent which led him to a trapped casualty."

Sheila — Collie
Date of Award: July 2, 1945

> "For assisting in the rescue of four American Airmen lost on the Cheviots in a blizzard after an air crash in December, 1944."

Rip — Mongrel
Stray picked up by Civil Defence Squad at Poplar, London E14
Date of Award: 1945

> "For locating many air-raid victims during the blitz of 1940."

Peter — Collie
Date of Award: November 1945

> "For locating victims trapped under blitzed buildings while serving with the MAP attached to Civil Defence of London."

Judy — Pedigree Pointer
Date of Award: May 1946

> "For magnificent courage and endurance in Japanese prison camps, which helped to maintain morale among her fellow prisoners and also for saving many lives through her intelligence and watchfulness."

Punch and Judy — Boxer dog and bitch
Date of Awards: November 1946

> "These dogs saved the lives of two British Officers in Israel by attacking an armed terrorist who was stealing upon them unawares and thus warning them of their danger. Punch

Peter with King George and Queen Elizabeth.

Punch, a boxer dog.

IN MEMORY OF
PUNCH DM
OWNED BY
LIEUTENANT COLONEL
A. H. K. CAMPBELL
DEPUTY JUDGE ADVOCATE GENERAL
OF THE JERUSALEM MILITARY COURT
AWARDED PDSA DICKIN MEDAL
NOVEMBER 1946
FOR SAVING THE LIVES OF
TWO BRITISH OFFICERS IN ISRAEL
BY ATTACKING AN ARMED TERRORIST
BURIED 7 DECEMBER 1954

sustained 4 bullet wounds and Judy a long graze down her back."

Ricky — Welsh Collie
Date of Award: March 29, 1947
"This dog was engaged in cleaning the verges of the canal bank at Nederweent, Holland. He found all the mines but during the operation one of them exploded. Ricky was wounded in the head but remained calm and kept at work. Had he become excited he would have been a danger to the rest of the section working nearby."

Brian — Alsatian
Date of Award: March 29, 1947
"This patrol dog was attached to a Parachute Battalion of the 13th Battalion Airborne Division. He landed in Normandy with them and, having done the requisite number of jumps, became a fully-qualified Paratrooper."

SERGEANT GANDER

Antis — Alsatian

Date of Award: January 28, 1949

"Owned by a Czech airman, this dog served with him in the French Air Force and RAF from 1940 to 1945, both in N. Africa and England. Returning to Czechoslovakia after the war, he substantially helped his master's escape across the frontier when after the death of Jan Masaryk, he had to fly from the Communists."

Tich — Egyptian Mongrel

1st Battalion King's Royal Rifle Corps

Date of Award: July 1, 1949

"For loyalty, courage and devotion to duty under hazardous conditions of war 1941 to 1945, while serving with the 1st King's Rifle Corps in North Africa and Italy."

Gander — Newfoundland

Date of Award: Awarded posthumously on October 27, 2000

"For saving the lives of Canadian infantrymen during the Battle of Lye Mun on Hong Kong Island in December 1941. On three documented occasions Gander, the Newfoundland mascot of the Royal Rifles of Canada engaged the enemy as his regiment joined the Winnipeg Grenadiers, members of Battalion Headquarters 'C' Force and other Commonwealth troops in their courageous defence of the Island. Twice Gander's attacks halted the enemy's advance and protected groups of wounded soldiers. In a final act of bravery the war dog was killed in action gathering a grenade. Without Gander's intervention many more lives would have been lost in the assault."

Appollo — German Shepherd

Date of Award: March 5, 2002

NYPD dog Appollo received the PDSA Dickin Medal on behalf of all the Search and Rescue dogs at Ground Zero and the Pentagon, following the terrorist attack on September 11, 2001.
"For tireless courage in the service of humanity during the search and rescue operations in New York and Washington on and after 11 September 2001. Faithful to words of command and undaunted by the task, the dog's work and unstinting devotion to duty stand as a testament to those lost or injured."

Salty and Roselle — Labrador guide dogs

Date of Award: March 5, 2002

Ricky's grave. Ricky was a little Welsh collie used in a mine-sweeping operation on a canal bank in Nederweent, Holland. He found all the mines, but was injured when one exploded. Ricky kept working despite his wounds.

"For remaining loyally at the side of their blind owners, courageously leading them down more than 70 floors of the World Trade Center and to a place of safety following the terrorist attack on New York on 11 September 2001."

Sam — German Shepherd
Royal Army Veterinary Corps
Date of Award: January 14, 2003

"For outstanding gallantry in April 1998 while assigned to the Royal Canadian Regiment in Drvar during the conflict in Bosnia-Hertzegovina. On two documented occasions Sam displayed great courage and devotion to duty. On 18 April Sam successfully brought down an armed man threatening the lives of civilians and Service personnel. On 24 April, while guarding a compound harbouring Serbian refugees, Sam's determined approach held off rioters until reinforcements arrived. This dog's true valour saved the lives of many servicemen and civilians during this time of human conflict."

Buster — Springer Spaniel
Royal Army Veterinary Corps
Date of Award: December 9, 2003

"For outstanding gallantry in March 2003 while assigned to the Duke of Wellington's Regiment in Safwan, Southern Iraq. Arms and explosives search dog Buster located an arsenal of weapons and explosives hidden behind a false wall in a property linked with an extremist group. Buster is considered responsible for saving the lives of service personnel and civilians. Following the find, all attacks ceased and shortly afterwards and troops replaced their steel helmets with berets."

Lucky — German Shepherd
RAF number 3610 AD: RAF Police anti-terrorist tracker dog — from 1949 to 1952 during the Malaya Campaign.
Date of Award: February 6, 2007

"For the outstanding gallantry and devotion to duty of the RAF Police anti-terrorist tracker dog team, comprising Bobbie, Jasper, Lassie and Lucky, while attached to the Civil Police and several British Army regiments including the Coldstream Guards, 2nd Battalion Royal Scots Guards and the Ghurkhas during the Malaya Campaign.
"Bobbie, Jasper, Lassie and Lucky displayed exceptional determination and life-saving skills during the Malaya Campaign. The dogs and their handlers were an exceptional team, capable of tracking and locating the enemy by scent despite unrelenting heat and an almost impregnable jungle. Sadly, three of the dogs lost their lives in the line of duty: only Lucky survived to the end of the conflict."

Sadie — Labrador
RAVC arms and explosive search dog — Kabul, Afghanistan in November 2005
Date of Award: February 6, 2007

> "For outstanding gallantry and devotion to duty while assigned to the Royal Gloucestershire, Berkshire and Wiltshire Light Infantry during conflict in Afghanistan in 2005. On 14 November 2005 military personnel serving with NATO's International Security Assistance Force in Kabul were involved in two separate attacks. Sadie and Lance Corporal Yardley were deployed to search for secondary explosive devices.

> "Sadie gave a positive indication near a concrete blast wall and multinational personnel were moved to a safe distance. Despite the obvious danger Sadie and Lance Corporal Yardley completed their search. At the site of Sadie's indication, bomb disposal operators later made safe an explosive device. The bomb was designed to inflict maximum injury. Sadie's actions undoubtedly saved the lives of many civilians and soldiers."

Pigeons

White Vision
Pigeon SURP.41.L.3089
Date of Award: December 2, 1943

> "For delivering a message under exceptionally difficult conditions and so contributing to the rescue of an Air Crew while serving with the RAF in October 1943."

Winkie
Pigeon NEHU.40.NS.1
Date of Award: December 2, 1943

> "For delivering a message under exceptionally difficult conditions and so contributing to the rescue of an Air Crew while serving with the RAF in February, 1942."

Tyke (also known as George)
Pigeon Number 1263 MEPS 43
Date of Award: December 2, 1943

> "For delivering a message under exceptionally difficult conditions and so contributing to the rescue of an Air Crew, while serving with the RAF in the Mediterranean in June, 1943."

Beach Comber
Pigeon NPS.41.NS.4230

Date of Award: March 6, 1944

"For bringing the first news to this country of the landing at Dieppe, under hazardous conditions in September, 1942, while serving with the Canadian Army."

Gustav
Pigeon NPS.42.31066
Date of Award: September 1, 1944

"For delivering the first message from the Normandy Beaches from a ship off the beach-head while serving with the RAF on 6 June 1944."

Paddy
Pigeon NPS.43.9451
Date of Award: September 1, 1944

"For the best recorded time with a message from the Normandy Operations, while serving with the RAF in June, 1944."

Kenley Lass
Pigeon NURP.36.JH.190
Date of Award: March 1945

"For being the first pigeon to be used with success for secret communications from an Agent in enemy-occupied France while serving with the NPS in October 1940."

Navy Blue
Pigeon NPS.41.NS.2862
Date of Award: March 1945

"For delivering an important message from a Raiding Party on the West Coast of France, although injured, while serving with the RAF in June, 1944.

Flying Dutchman
Pigeon NPS.42.NS.44802
Date of Award: March 1945

"For successfully delivering messages from Agents in Holland on three occasions. Missing on fourth mission, while serving with the RAF in 1944."

Dutch Coast
Pigeon NURP.41. A.2164
Date of Award: March 1945

"For delivering an SOS from a ditched Air Crew close to the enemy coast 288 miles distance in 7½ hours, under unfavourable conditions, while serving with the RAF in April 1942."

Commando
Pigeon NURP.38.EGU.242
Date of Award: March 1945
"For successfully delivering messages from Agents in Occupied France on three occasions: twice under exceptionally adverse conditions, while serving with the NPS in 1942."

Royal Blue
Pigeon NURP.40.GVIS.453
Date of Award: March 1945
"For being the first pigeon in this war to deliver a message from a forced landed aircraft on the Continent while serving with the RAF in October, 1940."

Ruhr Express
Pigeon NPS.43.29018
Date of Award: May 1945
"For carrying an important message from the Ruhr Pocket in excellent time, while serving with the RAF in April, 1945."

William of Orange
Pigeon NPS.42.NS.15125
Date of Award: May 1945
"For delivering a message from the Arnheim Airborne Operation in record time for any single pigeon, while serving with the APS in September 1944."

Scotch Lass
Pigeon NPS.42.21610
Date of Award: June 1945
"For bringing 38 microphotographs across the North Sea in good time although injured, while serving with the RAF in Holland in September 1944."

Billy
Pigeon NU.41.HQ.4373
Date of Award: August 1945
"For delivering a message from a force-landed bomber, while in a state of complete collapse and

under exceptionally bad weather conditions, while serving with the RAF in 1942."

Broad Arrow

Pigeon 41.BA.2793

Date of Award: October 1945

"For bringing important messages three times from enemy occupied country, viz: May 1943, June 1943 and August 1943, while serving with the Special Service from the Continent."

Pigeon NPS.42.NS.2780

Date of Award: October 1945

"For bringing important messages three times from enemy occupied country, viz: July 1942, August 1942 and April 1943, while serving with the Special Service from the Continent."

Pigeon NPS.42.NS.7524

Date of Award: October 1945

"For bringing important messages three times from enemy-occupied country, viz: July 1942, May 1943 and July 1943, while serving with the Special Service from the continent."

Maquis

Pigeon NPSNS.42.36392

Date of Award: October 1945

"For bringing important messages three times from enemy occupied country, viz: May 1943 (Amiens) February, 1944 (Combined Operations) and June, 1944 (French Maquis) while serving with the Special Service from the Continent."

Mary

Pigeon NURP.40.WCE.249

Date of Award: November 1945

"For outstanding endurance on War Service in spite of wounds."

Tommy

Pigeon NURP.41.DHZ56

Date of Award: February 1946

"For delivering a valuable message from Holland to Lancashire under difficult conditions, while serving with NPS in July 1942."

All Alone

Pigeon NURP.39.SDS.39

Date of Award: February 1946

> "For delivering an important message in one day over a distance of 400 miles, while serving with the NPS in August, 1943."

Princess

Pigeon 42WD593

Date of Award: May 1946

> "Sent on special mission to Crete, this pigeon returned to her loft (RAF Alexandria) having travelled about 500 miles mostly over sea, with most valuable information. One of the finest performances in the war record of the Pigeon Service."

Mercury

Pigeon NURP.37.CEN.335

Date of Award: August 1946

> "For carrying out a special task involving a flight of 480 miles from Northern Denmark while serving with the Special Section Army Pigeon Service in July 1942."

Pigeon NURP.38.BPC.6.

Date of Award: August 1946

> "For three outstanding flights from France while serving with the Special Section, Army Pigeon Service, 11 July 1941, 9 September 1941, and 29 November 1941."

GI Joe

Pigeon USA43SC6390

Date of Award: August 1946

> "This bird is credited with making the most outstanding flight by a USA Army Pigeon in World War II. Making the 20 mile flight from British 10th Army HQ, in the same number of minutes, it brought a message which arrived just in time to save the lives of at least 100 Allied soldiers from being bombed by their own planes."

Duke of Normandy

Pigeon NURP.41.SBC.219

Mary of Exeter.

Date of Award: January 8, 1947

> "For being the first bird to arrive with a message from Paratroops of 21st Army Group behind enemy lines on D Day 6 June, 1944, while serving with APS."

Pigeon NURP.43.CC.1418
Date of Award: January 8, 1947

> "For the fastest flight with message from 6th Airborne Div. Normandy, 7 June, 1944, while serving with APS."

Pigeon DD.43.T.139 (Australian Army Signal Corps)
Date of award: February 1947

> "During a heavy tropical storm this bird was released from Army Boat 1402 which had foundered on Wadou Beach in the Huon Gulf. Homing 40 miles to Madang it brought a message which enabled a rescue ship to be sent in time to salvage the craft and its valuable cargo of stores and ammunition."

Pigeon DD.43.Q.879 (Australian Army Signal Corps)
Date of award: February 1947

> "During an attack by Japanese on a US Marine patrol on Manus Island, pigeons were released to warn headquarters of an impending enemy counter-attack. Two were shot down but DD43 despite heavy fire directed at it reached HQ with the result that enemy concentrations were bombed and the patrol extricated."

Cologne
Pigeon NURP39.NPS.144
Date of Award: unknown

> "For homing from a crashed aircraft over Cologne although seriously wounded, while serving with the RAF in 1943."

Other Animals

Olga — Police Horse
Date of Award: April 11, 1947

> "On duty when a flying bomb demolished four houses in Tooting and a plate-glass window crashed immediately in front of her. Olga, after bolting for 100 yards, returned to the scene of the incident and remained on duty with her rider, controlling traffic and assisting rescue organizations."

Upstart — Police Horse
Date of Award: 11 April 1947

"While on patrol duty in Bethnal Green a flying bomb exploded within 75 yards, showering both horse and rider with broken glass and debris. Upstart was completely unperturbed and remained quietly on duty with his rider controlling traffic, etc., until the incident had been dealt with."

Regal — Police Horse
Date of Award: April 11, 1947

"Was twice in burning stables caused by explosive incendiaries at Muswell Hill. Although receiving minor injuries, being covered by debris and close to the flames, this horse showed no signs of panic."

Simon — Cat
Date of Award: awarded posthumously 1949

"Served on HMS *Amethyst* during the Yangtze Incident, disposing of many rats though wounded by shell blast. Throughout the incident his behaviour was of the highest order, although the blast was capable of making a hole over a foot in diameter in a steel plate."

Simon's grave.

Courtesy of Patrick Roberts, Purr'n'Fur.

Appendix B
List of "C" Force Royal Rifles

"C" Force — 1st Battalion of the Royal Rifles of Canada

NOTE: The information below is taken from the official DND Casualty Lists given to the General Public on 26 December 1941, following the Capture of Hong Kong. Some of the information, such as the individual's rank, may have changed while they were overseas.

Lieutenant Colonel:

Home, William James
Btn HQ
Quebec City, QC

Major:

Bishop, Wells Arnold
C Coy
Bury, QC

Macaulay, Malcom Thomas
    Gordon
HQ Coy
Bury, QC

Parker, Maurice Albert
D Coy
Sherbrooke, QC

Price, John Herbert
Btn HQ
Quebec City, QC

Young, Charles Alexander
A Coy
Quebec City, QC

Captain:

Atkinson, Frederick Temple
Btn HQ
Toronto, ON

Clarke, William Frank
HQ Coy
Quebec City, QC

Denison, Everette Ernest
B Coy
Danville, QC

Gavey, Joseph Charles
C Coy
Quebec City, QC

Hurd, Edmund Lionel
Btn HQ
Sherbrooke, QC

Leboutillier, William Percy Cecil
A Coy
Ottawa, ON

Price, Charles Edward
D Coy
Quebec City, QC

Royal, Frederick Henry James
B Coy
Montcalm, QC

Royal, Walter Allan Burt
HQ Coy
Danville, QC

Lieutenant:

Blaver, Collison Alexander
A Coy
Toronto, ON

Bradley, William Barker
C Coy
Quebec City, QC

Breakey, Ian
D Coy
Quebec City, QC

D'Avignon, Joseph Roger
    Edward
B Coy
Quebec City, QC

Denison, Elmer Norman
Coy unknown
Richmond, QC

Fry, William Scarth
HQ Coy
Westmount, QC

Johnston, Charles Douglas
A Coy
Quebec City, QC

Languedoc, Donald Bernard
HQ Coy
Westmount, QC

Lyster, Franklin Nelson
A Coy
South Durham, QC

MacDougall, Peter Lewis
HQ Coy
Montreal, QC

MacMillan, Angus Archibald
D Coy
Quebec City, QC

McGreevy, John Herbert
A Coy
La Malbaie, QC

Power, Francis Gavin
D Coy
Ottawa, ON

Ross, Francis Donald
Coy unknown
Quebec City, QC

Ross, James Forsyth
B Coy
Spencerwood, QC

Scott, Arthur Beresford
C Coy
Preston Park, QC

Simons, Reginald Ernest
D Coy
Quebec City, QC

Strang, Kenneth Ross
C Coy
Quebec City, QC

Thorn, Raymond Frank
B Coy
Quebec City, QC

Williams, Gerard Mott
HQ Coy
Quebec City, QC

Woodside, Arnold Rawlin Smith

Bde HQ
Quebec City, QC

Second Lieutenant:

Gilbert, James Cunningham
B Coy
Danville, QC

Smith, John Earle Denison
C Coy
Richmond, QC

Warrant Officer Class II:

Bilodeau, Albert
Regt # – P17154
Richelieu, QC

Ebdon, Frank William
Regt # – E29977
Valcartier, QC

Henderson, William Nelson
Regt # – E30088
Ville-Marie, QC

Kerrigan, Clifford Hatfield
Regt # – G17892
Aroostock, NB

Kirouac, Albert
Regt # – E22849
Quebec City, QC

Royea (Royer), Clifford Arnold
Regt # – E29813

Bury, QC

Shore, Leslie Walter
Regt # – E29809
River Bend, QC

Todd, Earl Crawford
Regt # – E22890
Bergerville, QC

Staff Sergeant:

Cole, Elmer William
Regt # – E30215
Sussex, NB

Laing, John Leslie
Regt # – F93451
Sherbrooke, NS

Macdonald, Lorne
Regt # – E30439
Scotstown, QC

Scott, Harold Charles
Regt # – G15004
Saint John, NB

Smith, Thomas William
Regt # – E29871
Drummondville, QC

Standish, Colin Alden
Regt # – E29812
Cookshire, QC

Thomson, John Brown

Regt # – E29806
Vancouver, BC

Wright, Stanley Walter
Regt # – E30021
Lachine, QC

Sergeant:

Beattie, Leonard A.
Regt # – A6146
Iberville, QC

Bernard, Emile Gregoire
Regt # – E30269
East Angus, QC

Brown, Andrew Herbert
Regt # – E29836
Danville, QC

Clark, Oswald Frank
Regt # – E29340
Bury, QC

Clarkson, Kenneth Herman
Regt # – E29901
Lacolle, QC

Clayton, Robert John
Regt # – B87788
Toronto, ON

Conway, Gordon Joseph
Regt # – E29856
East Angus, QC

Cronin, John Joseph
Regt # – E30104
Toronto, ON

Cuzner, John Garry
Regt # – E30029
Montreal, QC

D'Avignon, Maurice
Regt # – E30547
Marieville, QC

Doull, Lloyd Cissell
Regt # – E29875
Drummondville, QC

Gander
No Regt # – HQ Coy
Gander, NF

Hawke, William Dyson
Regt # – E197
Cowansville, QC

Hughes, Harold Branscombe
Regt # – B27145
Hamilton, ON

Jacobson, Tony Orville
Regt # – L50094
Norquay, SK

Macdonell, George Stuart
Regt # – A9220
Stratford, ON

MacMillan, James Clifford

Mitchell
Regt # – E30112
Campbellton, NB

Marshall, Albert William
Regt # – F29629
Halifax, NS

Martin, James
Regt # – E17046
Quebec City, QC

McNab, Lorne Richard
Regt # – E30081
Kenogami, QC

Parkes, Walter Raymond
Regt # – E29914
Richmond, QC

Pope, Colin Clifford
Regt # – E29818
Cookshire, QC

Pope, William Rufus
Regt # – E29819
Cookshire, QC

Richards, Thomas Medley
Regt # – E30185
Saint John, NB

Russell, Robert Leslie
Regt # – E22946
Quebec City, QC

Sauson, Lester Lawrence

Regt # – E29903
Shigawake, QC

Shepherd, Harold Barlow
Regt # – E30180
River Bend, QC

Simpson, Percy Leaman
Regt # – E29837
Rose Bridge, QC

Stickles, Leslie Robert
Regt # – E30270
Timmins, ON

Stoddard, Seldon Grant
Regt # – E30144
Waterloo, QC

Wilson, Thomas Woodrow
Regt # – E30231
Blacklands, NB

Wonnacott, Alfred
Regt # – E30243
Echo Bay, ON

Lance Sergeant:

Dissing, Eric Neils
Regt # – E30151
London, ON

Goodenough, Murray Thomas
Regt # – E21892
Bury, QC

McCarron, Joseph Maurice
Regt # – E29838
Harvey, NB

Pelletier, Percy Omar
Regt # – E30082
Donnacona, QC

Corporal:

Addie, Kenneth Gardner
Regt # – E29805
Quebec City, QC

Allen, William Harold
Regt # – E29952
East Angus, QC

Badger, James Edward
Regt # – E29923
Montreal, QC

Billson, Walter Gordon
Regt # – E29839
Lennoxville, QC

Brady, Charles Patrick
Regt # – E30233
Kenogabi, QC

Breen, Frederick
Regt # – E30299
Kirkland Lake, ON

Coleman, John Arthur
Regt # – E30060
Scotstown, QC

Collins, Alger Randolph
Regt # – E30129
Albert, NB

Cook, James Alfred
Regt # – E21900
Bury, QC

Dobb, William Orie
Regt # – E29851
Sherbrooke, QC

Doull, Llewellyn Thomas
    Sydney
Regt # – E29873
Drummondville, QC

Fitzpatrick, John Joseph
Regt # – E21822
Quebec City, QC

Fletcher, Charles William
Regt # – E30282
Lake Megantic, QC

Gee, John Moffet
Regt # – G32406
Birch Ridge, NB

Gibbs, Douglas A. Robert
Regt # – E29961
Melbourne, QC

Grant, Richard Joseph
Regt # –E30275
New Richmond, QC

Harlow, William Joseph
Regt # –E29934
Cookshire, QC

Jessop, Albert Fred
Regt # – E30197
Edmundston, NB

Johnson, John Seward
Regt # – G18276
Sackville, NB

Latimer, Lorne Rayburn
Regt # – E30092
Detroit, MI, USA

Macaulay, Cecil Kenneth
Regt # – E30314
Scotstown, QC

MacIsaac, John Jamiseson
Regt # – E30370
Judique North, NS

MacNaughton, William
Regt # – E29963
Matapedia, QC

Macrae, Allan Howard
Regt # – E30053
Scotstown, QC

Martel, George Henry
Regt # – E30216
Quebec City, QC

McClellan, Wendell

Regt # – E30321
New Westminster, BC

Mcrae, George William
Regt # – E29951
Chandler, QC

Moores, Mortimer
Regt # – E30453
Matapedia, QC

Nicholson, Harold Frank
Regt # – F93468
Montague, PEI

Nolan, Alex Richard
Regt # – E30436
Loggieville, NB

Phillips, Edward
Regt # – E30244
Sawyerville, QC

Pollock, Charles James William
Regt # – E30332
Glen Levit, NB

Porter, Jack
Regt # – B40638
Niagara Falls, ON

Roberts, Austin James
Regt # – E30123
Glen Levit, NB

Roberts, Melvin
Regt # – E29898

Peninsula, QC

Robitaille, Gaudiose
Regt # – E22880
Quebec West, QC

Robson, Arthur Taylor
Regt # – E29899
Kenogami, QC

Rose, Albert
Regt # – E29967
Joint A La Garde, QC

Ross, Lancelot Scott
Regt # – E1144
Paspebiac, QC

Sauson, Edward Lewis
Regt # – E29904
Shigawake, QC

Sauson, Oliver Ray
Regt # – E29902
Shigawake, QC

Savage, Carlyle Fitch
Regt # – F40262
Berwick, NS

Smith, Elmer Clifford
Regt # – F40510
Scotsburn, NS

Stoddard, Raymond
Regt # – E30609
Cookshire, QC

Syvret, Dempsey Aaron
Regt # – E29979
Gaspe, QC

Vermett, Patrick
Regt # – E30451
Campbellton, NB

Walsh, James Stanford
Regt # – E30405
Entry Island, QC

Wood, Leonard George
Regt # – E30191
Lac Megantic, QC

Lance Corporal

Adams, David Morland
Regt # – G27650
Matapedia, QC

Barter, Robert Burns
Regt # – E29987
Grand Cascapedia, QC

Brazel, Ervin Arnold
Regt # – E30466
Birchton, QC

Cameron, Floyd Colin
Regt # – E30608
Sawyerville, QC

Campbelton, Edward Albert
Regt # – E30072
Asbestos, QC

Chenell, James Maxwell
Regt # – E30406
Magdalen Islands, QC

Dallain, Charles Claude
Regt # – E30434
New Carlisle, QC

Day, Frederick
Regt # – E29861
New Carlisle, QC

Enright, Arley
Regt # – E30255
Hopetown, QC

Fair, Gray John
Regt # – E29982
Pointe a la Garde, QC

Fallow, William
Regt # – E29136
New Richmond, QC

Farace, Paul
Regt # – B40577
Toronto, ON

Findlay, George Knox
Regt # – E29844
Danville, QC

Gillis, Malcom
Regt # – E30041
Runnymede, QC

Harrison, Argyle Clayton

Regt # – E30067
Bury, QC

Harrison, Edwin
Regt # – E29957
Grand Cascapedia, QC

Heath, Harold Simon
Regt # – E29840
Danville, QC

Heath, James Graydon
Regt # – E29915
Danville, QC

Henderson, Walter Charles
Regt # - E30429
Waterloo, QC

Ladds, Ernest George
Regt # – E30090
Noranda, QC

Lapointe, Valmore
Regt # – E30311
Riviere du Loup, QC

Little, Orval Louis
Regt # – A44514
Athens, GA, USA

Lowe, Donald
Regt # – E30134
Giraudais, QC

Macpherson, John Francis
Regt # – F40747

Wolfville, NB

Mann, Lindsay Richard
Regt # – E30014
Runnymede, QC

Matchett, Eugene Boyd
Regt # – E30232
Sunny Corner, NB

McLean, James Patton
Regt # – E30407
Entry Island, QC

Meredith, Eddie
Regt # – E29955
Montreal, QC

Miller, David Ross
Regt # – E30613
Wakeham, QC

Mulcahy, Patrick Francis
Regt # – P48688
Quebec City, QC

Mulrooney, Quentin
Regt # – E29884
Douglastown, QC

Nicholson, Malcom
Regt # – E29928
Scotstown, QC

Nicol, Noble
Regt # – E30110
Sellarsville, QC

Palmer, George Thomas
Regt # – F40192
St. Peter's Bay, PEI

Patton, Herbert Borden
Regt # – E30183
St. John's, NL

Perreault, Arthur
Regt # – E29906
Fontenelle, QC

Rodrigues, Edwin
Regt # – E30694
Bosseterre, St. Kitts, BWI

Sannes, Aksel George Andersen
Regt # – E30324
Campbellton, NB

Simpson, Harry Cyril
Regt # – E29872
Drummondville, QC

Somerville, Reginald David
Regt # – E22886
Bergerville, QC

Southgate, Marcus
Regt # – E29850
Sherbrooke, QC

Travers, Charles Wilson
Regt # – E30188
Sault Ste. Marie, ON

Rifleman:

Acorn, John Murdock
Regt # – F40906
Deer Lake, ON

Acorn, Joseph Amon
Regt # – F40903
Peter's Road, PEI

Adams, Bryce Harold
Regt # – E30135
Millstream, QC

Adams, Carl
Regt # – E30677
Hamilton, ON

Adams, Harry Vernon
Regt # – E30238
Campbellton, QC

Adams, Lawrence Leonard
Regt # – A4240
Kitchener, ON

Adams, Raymond Lee
Regt # – E30120
Campbellton, NB

Aitken, Deighton
Regt # – E30391
Magdalen Islands, QC

Aitkens, Edward Carlton
Regt # – E30383
Magdalen Islands, QC

Aksenchuk, Jerry Tony

Regt # – B68229
Carrick, MB

Alden, Arthur Clayton
Regt # – E30045
Island Brook, NF

Allen, Irvin
Regt # – E29921
Windsor Mills, QC

Allen, Louis
Regt # – E30199
St. Zacherie, QC

Allen, Peter Joseph
Regt # – G18311
Summerville, MA, USA

Alley, Ralph Donald
Regt # – C40670
Trent River, ON

Allison, Seymour George
Regt # – E30136
Escuminac, QC

Ampi, Kalle
Regt # – F30594
Quebec City, QC

Andrews, Albert Lorne
Regt # – E30262
Lac Megantic, QC

Antilla, Leo Sikstus
Regt # – E30276

Kenogami, QC

Archibald, Alexander
Regt # – E30249
Kenogami, QC

Archibald, James
Regt # – C65411
Port Hope, ON

Archibald, James Wallace
Regt # – E30340
Fredericton, NB

Arno, Frank
Regt # – E30295
Whiteney, ON

Arsenault, Alfred
Regt # – E30704
Campbellton, NB

Arsenault, Andrew
Regt # – E30420
Athoville, NB

Arseneau, Andrew Joseph
Regt # – E30132
Upsaiquitch, NB

Arseneau, Jules
Regt # – E30133
Adams Gulch, NB

Arseneault, Sylvere
Regt # – E30273
Atholville, NB

Arthur, Jack
Regt # – E30418
Oshawa, ON

Atwood, Percy
Regt # – F40870
Barrington, NS

Aumont, George Frank
Regt # – B4483
Barrie, ON

Babcock, Floyd Glover
Regt # – E30099
Broadlands, QC

Babin, Alfred Joseph
Regt # – G27036
Sydney, NS

Bacon, Laureat
Regt # – E30652
Quebec City, QC

Baker, George W. Harold
Regt # – E30200
Scotstown, QC

Baker, Harold Albert
Regt # – E29848
Compton, QC

Baker, John Vincent
Regt # – C40665
Campbellford, ON

Bannister, Kenneth Harry

Regt # – G15013
Saint John, NB

Barclay, Robert McMillan
Regt # – E30417
Durham Centre, NB

Barclay, William John
Regt # – E30450
Tidehead, NB

Barnes, Kenneth
Regt # – E30117
Escuminac, QC

Barnett, Clifford Gerald
Regt # – B64068
Toronto, ON

Barrieault, Albert Harold
Regt # – E30236
Maria East, QC

Barron, George
Regt # – B75072
Baltimore, ON

Baskin, John Angus
Regt # – E30513
Blacklands, NB

Bate, Ernest
Regt # – E30301
Maxelsfield, British Isles

Batley, Austin Guy
Regt # – E30153

Bury, QC

Batley, Eric Aubrey
Regt # – E30155
Bury, QC

Beacroft, Ronald Robert
Regt # – B87858
Unknown, ON

Beattie, Kenneth Graham
Regt # – E30758
Richmond, QC

Bedard, Rene Napoleon
Regt # – E30066
Sawyerville, QC

Beebe, Jack
Regt # – E30258
Port Daniel, QC

Bennett, Ernest Irwin
Regt # – E30245
Bury, QC

Bent, Howard Norman
Regt # – F40829
Halifax, NS

Benwell, Marvin
Regt # – E30699
Marcil, QC

Bernier, Donat
Regt # – E30318
Warwick, QC

Berthelot, Delphis Girard
Regt # – E30131
St. Jean L'Evangeliste, QC

Bertin, Edmund
Regt # – E30506
New Mills, NB

Best, William
Regt # – E29948
Grand Cascapedia, QC

Bevan, Clarence Frederick
Regt # – C65245
Coburg, ON

Bisson, George Stanislas
Regt # – E30281
Paspebiac, QC

Blacquiere, Joseph Medius
Regt # – F40905
Nauwigewauk, NB

Blanchard, Albenie
Regt # – E30222
Val D'Amour, NB

Blanchette, Emile
Regt # – E30139
Indian Cove, QC

Blank, Elmer Walter
Regt # – E30291
Seven Sisters Falls, MB

Blaquiere, Clement

Regt # – E199
Atholville, NB

Boissonneault, Adrien Emile
Regt # – E29823
Danville, QC

Bolton, Edward Charles
Regt # – B38358
Oshawa, ON

Bond, Eugene
Regt # – E29881
Barachois, QC

Bottie, Leo Joseph
Regt # – F41001
West Lardoise, NS

Boudreau, John Graham
    Dumont
Regt # – E30380
Glen Levit, NB

Boudreau, John Wendall
Regt # – E30220
Balmoral, NB

Boudreau, Robert Andrew
    Augustine
Regt # – E30377
Glen Levit, NB

Boudreau, Sylvestre
Regt # – E30474
St. Jules de Maria, QC

Boudreau, Vance
Regt # – E30623
Glen Levit, NB

Boulanger, Benoit Eugene
Regt # – E30480
Montreal, QC

Bouley, Narcisse
Regt # – E30705
Campbellton, NB

Bourget, Ernest
Regt # – E30493
Cape Cove, QC

Bourget, Robert
Regt # – E30631
Perce, QC

Boutin, Marius
Regt # – E29807
Breakyville, QC

Bowerbank, Frank Eric
Regt # – B38342
Hamilton, ON

Briand, Rannie
Regt # – E29887
Douglastown, QC

Briard, Alfred Jean Baptiste
Regt # – E30567
Peninsula, QC

Brine, Frederick Alfred

Regt # – G18270
Port Elgin, NB

Brophy, Bernard Francis
Regt # – E30650
Frederick, WS, USA

Brown, Louis
Regt # – B68230
Toronto, ON

Brown, Murray Blair
Regt # – E30577
Hampton, NB

Buchanan, Hercules Ralph
Regt # – F40923
Lockeport, NS

Buckley, George
Regt # – E30087
Bridgeville, QC

Bujold, Hubert
Regt # – E30171
Cross Point, QC

Bujold, John Edward
Regt # – E30145
Cross Point, QC

Bujold, Joseph John
Regt # – E30142
Fleurant Pointe, QC

Bujold, Ludovic
Regt # – E30519

Charlo, QC

Bujold, Paul
Regt # - E30178
Cross Pointe, QC

Burgess, Walter James
Regt # – C57530
Cornwall, ON

Burns, John Francis
Regt # – C5842
Hartford, CT, USA

Burns, Peter Crombie
Regt # – B38357
Hamilton, ON

Burton, Woodburn Keith
Regt # – E30727
New Richmond, QC

Butler, Gerard Patrick
Regt # – G17847
Saint John, NB

Cadoret, Bruce
Regt # – E30538
Bougainville, QC

Calder, George
Regt # – E30102
Broadlands, QC

Calder, Vincent Archie
Regt # – B46619
Hamilton, ON

Cambon, Kenneth
Regt # – E22967
Quebec City, QC

Campbell, Charlie George
Regt # – E30644
Grand Cascapedia, QC

Campbell, John Langemarcke
Regt # – B74967
Elmvale, ON

Campbell, Kenneth Alexander
Regt # – B68202
Collingwood, ON

Campbell, Ralph Wesley
Regt # – E30471
Campbellton, NB

Campbell, William Robert
Regt # – B75063
Novar, ON

Cardin, Waldorf Joseph
Regt # – E30692
Drummondville, QC

Caron, Michel Ormendy
Regt # – E30478
L'Anse au Beaufils, QC

Carr, Ashton Frederick
Regt # – G18689
Doaktown, NB

Carr, Murray Garnet

Regt # – G27223
Sussex, NB

Carter, Melbourne John
    Jefferson
Regt # – B74256
Toronto, ON

Castonguay, Bernard
Regt # – E30659
Montreal, QC

Chalmers, Ralph Kingston
Regt # – B68234
Thornhill, ON

Chambers, Donald Murray
Regt # – G27224
Elgin, NB

Chanberlain, Robert
Regt # – E30628
Campbellton, NB

Chapados, Romain
Regt # – E30298
Paspeblac, QC

Chapman, Frank
Regt # – E29935
Bury, QC

Chapman, Frederick Orland
Regt # – E30553
Orillia, ON

Chard, John Frederick

Regt # – C65282
Toronto, ON

Chatterton, Orrin James
Regt # – E29830
Carlisle, QC

Chenell, Albert Benjamin
Regt # – E30392
Magdalen Islands, QC

Chenell, Bernard Leslie
Regt # – E30389
Magdalen Islands, QC

Chenell, Edward Bahan
Regt # – E30403
Magdalen Islands, QC

Chenell, George Borden
Regt # – E30379
Magdalen Islands, QC

Chenell, William Bradley
Regt # – E30381
Magdalen Islands, QC

Chesser, Charles Henry
Regt # – E30040
Matapedia, QC

Chesser, Kenneth
Regt # – E30013
Matapedia, QC

Chicoine, Gaston
Regt # – E30495

Barachois, QC

Chicoine, Herbert
Regt # – E29905
Barachois, QC

Churchill, Greorge Ralph
Regt # – F43639
Sandford, NS

Clapperton, Albert George
Regt # – E30266
Grand Cascapedia, QC

Claricoates, Ronald
Regt # – E30161
Bosworth, British Isles

Clarke, Charles Henry
Regt # – E30402
Magdalen Islands, QC

Clarke, George
Regt # – E30768
Arnprior, ON

Coates, Russell
Regt # – E30154
Bury, QC

Cochrane, Charles Angus
Regt # – E29954
New Richmond, QC

Coffin, Ninian Allan
Regt # – E30459
Gaspe Harbour, QC

Cole, Bliss Thomas
Regt # –E30079
Sussex, NB

Cole, Lewis Alfred
Regt # – E30557
Turtle Creek, NB

Cole, Lloyd Kerr
Regt # – E30529
Campbellton, NB

Coleman, Glen Myron
Regt # – E30063
Scotstown, QC

Coleman, Ralph George
Regt # – E30062
Bury, QC

Comeau, Bert
Regt # – E30202
Barachois, QC

Comeau, Isaac
Regt # – G18268
Maltempeque, NB

Comeau, Martin Joseph
Regt # – E30350
Campbellton, QC

Commerford, Patrick
Regt # – E22816
Quebec City, QC

Conron, Gordon James

Regt # – B68241
Toronto, ON

Cooper, Frederick Arthur
Regt # – B68226
Sutton West, ON

Cormier, Frank
Regt # – E29950
Amherst, NS

Cormier, Leo Abbey
Regt # – G18272
Gaspe Harbour, QC

Cormier, Norman Joseph
Regt # – E30346
Black Point, NB

Cote, Elisee
Regt # – E30637
South Durham, QC

Cotton, Leonard
Regt # – E30603
Flatlands, NB

Coughlan, Peter Gordon
Regt # – E30230
Pointe A La Garde, QC

Coughler, Wendell Ferguson
Regt # – C31402
Morrisburg, ON

Coull, Blair Stewart
Regt # – E30770

Grand Cascapedia, QC

Coull, John Arnold
Regt # – E30771
Grand Cascapedia, QC

Courier, Joseph Arnold
Regt # – E30526
Culligan, NB

Court, James Gordon
Regt # – E30734
West Hill, ON

Court, Kenneth Arnold
Regt # – E30126
Escuminac, QC

Court, William Henry
Regt # – E30160
Escuminac, QC

Craig, Bryce Huntley
Regt # – E29820
Matane County, QC

Crook, Wilfred Henry
Regt # – E30084
Richmond, QC

Crosman, Philip George
Regt # - E29866
Little Pabos, QC

Culleton, Edward
Regt # – E30149
Matapedia, QC

Culleton, Wellington
Regt # – E30039
Matapedia, QC

Cunning, Leslie
Regt # – E30612
Gaspe, QC

Cyr, Adolphe
Regt # – E30371
New Richmond, QC

Cyr, Augustin
Regt # – E30357
New Richmond, QC

Cyr, Clement
Regt # – E30414
New Richmond, QC

Cyr, Euclide
Regt # – E30365
New Richmond, QC

Cyr, Leon
Regt # – E30355
New Richmond, QC

Cyr, Roger
Regt # – E30726
New Richmond, QC

Cyr, Theophile
Regt # – E30361
New Richmond, QC

Cyr, Willmer Joseph

Regt # – E30426
Noranda, QC

Daigle, Edgar
Regt # – E30648
Campbellton, NB

Dainard, Donald
Regt # – C65333
Campbellford, ON

Dallain, Paul John
Regt # – E30264
New Carlisle, QC

Dancause, Paul
Regt # – E29924
Richmond, QC

Danyluck, Nicholas
Regt # – E30094
Black Donald, ON

Darrah, James Cornelius
Regt # – G18485
West Glassville, NB

Davidson, Alvin James
Regt # – E29846
Sawyerville, QC

Davidson, Earl Edwin
Regt # – E29857
Drummondville, QC

Davies, Morgan Isaac
Regt # – E30077

Norand, QC
Dawe, Kenneth Frederick
Regt # – D77280
Verdun, QC

Day, William George
Regt # – E29971
Escuminac, QC

De Vouge, Alva Vernon
Regt # – E30680
Belle Anse, QC

De Vouge, Cecil James
Regt # – E29892
Gaspe, QC

Dee, Nicholas
Regt # – E30358
New Richmond, QC

Delaney, Alexander Ryan
Regt # – E30573
Matapedia, QC

Delaney, Joseph
Regt # – E30320
House Harbour, QC

Delaney, Morris
Regt # – E29123
New Carlisle, QC

Delarosbil, Pierre Lionel
Regt # – E30766
Paspebiac, QC

Demers, Emile
Regt # – E30162
Drummondville, QC

Dempsey, Joseph Anthony Lyle
Regt # – E30515
Jacquet River, NB

Dewey, Ralph Atrol
Regt # – B74345
Toronto, ON

Di Sensi, Samuel
Regt # – E30605
Montreal, QC

Dixon, Alfred Armstrong
Regt # – B64580
Toronto, ON

Doddridge, Philip
Regt # – E29986
New Richmond, QC

Doiron, John Leo
Regt # – F40908
Hope River, PEI

Doiron, Leonard
Regt # – E29966
Matapedia, QC

Doiron, Marcel Joseph Jean-
    Marie
Regt # – E30285
Matapedia, QC

Doody, Irving Garnet
Regt # – E30678
Bougainville, QC

Doran, Alexander
Regt # – E30747
Newcastle, NB

Dorion, Rosaire
Regt # – E10206
Gaspe, QC

Doucet, Edgar
Regt # – E30317
West Bathurst, NB

Doucett, Peter
Regt # – G18332
Jardinville, QC

Doucette, Gerald Henry
Regt # – F42586
Botwood, NL

Dow, Ronald
Regt # – E30252
Marcil, QC

Dow, William Elwood
Regt # – E29897
Port Daniel, QC

Doyle, Joseph Leonard
Regt # – E29814
Montreal, QC

Driscole, Abraham

Regt # – E30356
Sunnyside, NB

Drouin, Raymond
Regt # – E30717
Quebec City, QC

Drover, Archibald Frederick
Regt # – E30730
St. John's, NL

Dubois, Leo Peter
Regt # – E30057
Sawyerville, QC

Duggan, Arthur Gray
Regt # – E30080
Kenogami, QC

Duguay, Joseph Aubin
Regt # – E30393
St. Arthur, NB

Dunlop, Robert Harold
Regt # – A11998
Stratford, ON

Duplassie, Bernard Patrick
Regt # – E30530
Upper Hills, NB

Dupont, Elroy George
Regt # – C65633
Pembroke, ON

Durant, Ferdinand Wilson
Regt # – E29874

Jonquiere, QC

Durdle, Robert
Regt # – E30731
Bonavista, NL

Edgecombe, George E
Regt # – B68236
Toronto, ON

Elliott, Raymond
Regt # – E30023
Pointe A La Garde, QC

Elsliger, Alfred William
Regt # – E30574
Jacquet River, NB

Englehart, Harold Wilfred
Regt # – E30175
Wyer's Brook, NB

Englehart, Rupert Charles
Regt # – E29983
Wyer's Brook, NB

Evans, Francis Henry
Regt # - B46009
Kingston, ON

Evans, Joseph Erwin
Regt # - E30762
Asbestos, QC

Everett, George Thomas
Regt # – E30158
Bury, QC

Ewing, Kenneth Alexander
Regt # – E30578
Hampton, NB

Fehr, Victor Oliver
Regt # – B68310
Niagara Falls, ON

Ferguson, George Alfred
Regt # – F16319
Montreal, QC

Ferrigan, John Thomas
Regt # – E30294
Campbell's Bay, QC

Findlay, Lorne Clifton Raymond
Regt # – E30763
Asbestos, QC

Findley, Joseph
Regt # – E29925
Stourbridge, England

Finn, Eli
Regt # – E29885
L'Anse a Brilliant, QC

Firlotte, James Blair
Regt # – E30016
Durham Centre, NB

Firlotte, John Fidell
Regt # – E30508
Bathurst, NB

Firlotte, Lawrence Joseph

Regt # – E30212
Campbellton, NB

Firlotte, Leslie Joseph
Regt # – E30347
Campbellton, NB

Firth, Denzil John George
Regt # – E30325
Matapedia, QC

Firth, Malcolm
Regt # – E30735
Dawsonville, NB

Fitzpatrick, Charles John Fitz
Regt # – E30684
Quebec City, QC

Fitzpatrick, John Joseph
Regt # – E21822
Quebec City, QC

Flanagan, Clifford Allison
Regt # - E30169
Dalhousie, NB

Flanagan, James Andrew
Regt # – E30353
Jacquet River, NB

Fleming, Robert James
Regt # – B38364
Toronto, ON

Flowers, Alexander
Regt # – E30469

New Carlylie, QC

Forsyth, Delmar William
Regt # – E29910
Chicoutimi, QC

Forsyth, Robert
Regt # – B40795
Pittsburgh, PA, USA

Francis, Earl Foch
Regt # – F35248
Halifax, NS

Fraser, Cameron D
Regt # – E30032
Matapedia, QC

Fredette, Hormidas
Regt # – E29827
Richmond, QC

Frenette, Joseph Charles
Regt # – E30329
Glen Levit, QC

Frost, Kenneth Ivan
Regt # – E30280
Asbestos, QC

Gagne, William Harvey
Regt # – C40614
Brighton, ON

Galbraith, Henry Robert
Regt # – C65590
Oshawa, ON

Gallagher, Frank Baker
Regt # – E29984
Maria East, QC

Gallant, Benjamin John
(Joseph)
Regt # – E30335
Glencoe, NB

Gallant, Clement
Regt # – E30170
Cross Point, QC

Gallant, Joseph Francis
Regt # – E30398
Glencoe, NB

Gallaway, William Edward
Regt # – C34054
Cumberland, ON

Gallie, Phillip James MacMillan
Regt # – E30341
Blacklands, NB

Gallon, John Wesley
Regt # – E30522
Black Point, NB

Gammack, Maurice
Regt # – E29860
Cromlet Bank, Scotland

Gates, Kenneth Harlon
Regt # – F40937
Kentville, NS

Gaudin, Kenneth Mearl
Regt # – E30229
Escuminac, QC

Gauthier, John A
Regt # – A23075
Detroit, MI, USA

Gendron, Laurier
Regt # – E30614
Montreal, QC

Geraghty, Donald
Regt # – B45551
Hamilton, ON

Geraghty, Oliver
Regt # – E30118
Oak Bay Mills, QC

Gerard, George Thomas
Regt # – G22736
St. Alexis, QC

Gibbons, Harold Earl
Regt # – A44596
Southampton, ON

Gignac, Louis
Regt # – E30620
Campbellton, NB

Gilbert, Bertam Scott
Regt # – E30074
Marbelton, QC

Gillis, Archie Peter

Regt # – E30289
Judique North, NS

Girard, Alex
Regt # – E29908
Barachois, QC

Glendenning, Harry Eldon
Regt # – E30481
South Bathurst, NB

Glenn, John Eric
Regt # – C40531
Trenton, ON

Gover, Ronald Albert
Regt # – B38359
South River, ON

Graham, Albert George
Regt # – B40622
Niagara Falls, ON

Graves, Arnold
Regt # – E30071
Anagance, NB

Gray, Gordon Alexander
Regt # – E30241
Bury, QC

Gray, Howard Warden
Regt # – E30050
Bury, QC

Gray, Walter Scott
Regt # – E30101

Fleurant Point, QC

Green, Wallace Sidney
Regt # – B87802
Toronto, ON

Gregoire, Glenford Robert
Regt # – B30177
Broadlands, QC

Grey, Walter
Regt # – C65160
Toronto, ON

Grieves, Richard Norman
Regt # – C65364
Haliburton, ON

Grieves, Willis John
Regt # – C65378
Campbellford, ON

Grimshaw, George
Regt # – D71020
Montreal, QC

Guitard, Gabriel
Regt # – E30503
Nash Creek, NB

Gunter, Murlin
Regt # – E30302
South Durham, QC

Guthrie, George Graham
Regt # – E29909
Montreal, QC

Guthrie, James
Regt # – E29911
Montreal, QC

Hachey, Dean William
Regt # – E38184
Atholville, NB

Hachey, Gerald
Regt # – E30416
West Bathurst, QC

Haley, Bernard
Regt # – E30005
Matapedia, QC

Haley, Reginald
Regt # – E29999
Matapedia, QC

Halley, George
Regt # – E30056
Bury, QC

Hamilton, Sterling Waldo
Regt # – E30113
Campbellton, NB

Hamilton, Wordsworth Wilmet
Regt # – E30527
Blacklands, NB

Hamon, Lionel Joseph
Regt # – E30488
Gaspe, QC

Hand, Jason Howell

Regt # – A20525
Verdun, QC

Hannan, Patrick Arthur Joseph
Regt # – E30422
Richmond, QC

Hanson, Clayton Andrew
Regt # – M61817
Pouce Coupe, BC

Harding, Bertie John
Regt # – E30775
Bergerville, QC

Harding, Robert Wilber
Regt # – E30713
Andover, MA, USA

Hardy, Joseph Ralston
Regt # – E30723
New Richmond, QC

Harper, Allen Ross
Regt # – B68233
Stouffville, ON

Harris, James Mistie
Regt # – E30472
Campbellton, NB

Harrison, Edmond Cameron
Regt # – E29926
Bury, QC

Harrison, Otis Maxwell
Regt # – E30769

Grand Cascapedia, QC

Hartery, Edward John
Regt # – E30737
St. John's, NL

Hay, Clarence Victor
Regt # – C40669
Campbellford, ON

Hebert, Raymond Joseph
Regt # – C41288
Renfrew, ON

Hellsten, Einar
Regt # – E30277
Kenogami, QC

Henderson, Elzie Joseph
Regt # – C65065
Haliburton, ON

Henderson, Gerald
Regt # – E30096
Maniwaki, QC

Henderson, Lawrence
Regt # – E29960
Richmond, QC

Henderson, Norman Ruderford
Regt # – B63743
Toronto, ON

Henderson, Stewart Derrill
Regt # – E29919
Richmond, QC

Henry, Thomas Raymond
Regt # – E30475
Campbellton, NB

Herman, John James
Regt # – E30499
Lintoilou, QC

Herring, Elwin Eric
Regt # – E40416
Bury, QC

Hickey, Charles Gordon
Regt # – E30517
Nask Creek, NB

Hickey, Joseph Sydney
Regt # – E30516
Windsor, ON

Hickey, Paul Joseph Henry
Regt # – E30514
Nask Creek, NB

Hickie, William Joseph
Regt # - E30331
Nask Creek, NB

Hicks, Frank
Regt # – A23006
Kingsville, ON

Holstock, William Harold
Regt # – B68217
Sutton West, ON

Hopgood, Leslie Revelle

Regt # – B68238
Weston, ON

Horwwell, George Herbert
Regt # – B72702
Toronto, ON

Hotton, Bertam Nelson
Regt # – E22611
Barachois, QC

Hotton, John Ivan
Regt # – E22610
Belle Anse, QC

Hunchuck, Harold
Regt # – B68203
Weston, ON

Hunt, Alfred
Regt # – E30748
Chandler, QC

Hunt, Clarence James
Regt # – E29342
Bury, QC

Hunt, Hector
Regt # – E29865
Quebec City, QC

Hunt, Joseph Arnold
Regt # – E29864
Chandler, QC

Huntington, Ralph
Regt # – E30261

New Carlisle, QC

Huntington, Windom
Regt # – E30751
Hope Town, QC

Hutchinson, Gordon T
Regt # – E30570
Norton, NB

Inche, Kenneth Ronald
Regt # – C65559
Oshawa, ON

Ingalls, Keith Campbell
Regt # – E29833
Cowansville, QC

Innes, Donald George
Regt # – B38350
Hunts, ON

Innes, Karl Silver
Regt # – B30728
St. Johns, NL

Iriel, Daniel
Regt # – B68173
Unknown

Irvine, Bertram
Regt # – E30002
Flatlands, NB

Irvine, Crandel
Regt # – E30042
Mann Settlement, QC

Irvine, Glenford
Regt # – E30172
Flatlands, QC

Irvine, Gordon
Regt # – E30043
Mann Settlement, QC

Irvine, Harold John
Regt # – E30148
Campbellton, NB

Irvine, James Donald
Regt # – E30001
Matapedia, QC

Irvine, James Maxwell
Regt # – G22769
Matapedia, QC

Irvine, John Barney
Regt # – E30036
Matapedia, QC

Irvine, Richard Maxwell
Regt # – G22746
Mann's Settlement, QC

Irvine, Ronald
Regt # – E30033
Unknown

Irving, Morton Alexander
Regt # – E30221
Matapedia, QC

Irving, Westley

Regt # – E30326
Flatlands, NB

Jackson, Ray Donald
Regt # – B68205
Chesley, ON

Jacquard, Angus John
Regt # – F42667
Little River Harbour, NS

Jacquard, Gilbert George
Regt # – F40912
Comeaus Hill, NS

Jacques, Daniel
Regt # – E29883
Fontenelle, QC

Jacques, Israel
Regt # – E29891
Gaspe, QC

Jamieson, David Allen
Regt # – C41269
Renfrew, ON

Jessop, James Robert
Regt # – E30584
Edmundston, NB

Jewers, Alton Edwarde
Regt # – F35214
Halifax, NS

Jiggins, Frank
Regt # – C65439

Port Hope, ON

Johnson, Leo
Regt # – E30632
West Bathhurst, NB

Jones, Thomas George
Regt # – C41279
Pembrooke, ON

Joseph, Alexandre
Regt # – E30256
Pasperee, QC

Josey, Ancil Lloyd
Regt # - E30390
Magdalen Islands, QC

Kaine, Eursal
Regt # – E30003
Mann Settlement, QC

Kaine, John
Regt # – E30211
Mann Settlement, QC

Kane, Michael John
Regt # – A20387
Renfrew, ON

Keating, Edward Ross
Regt # – B68171
Toronto, ON

Keays, Albert Clinton
Regt # – E30115
Escuminac North, QC

Keays, Richard
Regt # – E30657
Broadlands, QC

Kellaway, Gordon Garnet
Regt # – B74350
Lansing, ON

Kelly, Frederick Joseph
Regt # – E30520
Campbellton, NB

Kelso, Allen
Regt # – E29936
Bury, QC

Kelso, John
Regt # – E29815
Montreal, QC

Kendall, Donald
Regt # – E30187
Windsor Mills, ON

Kerr, Stephen Maxwell
Regt # – F40849
Port Williams, NS

Killoran, John Micheal
Regt # – E30507
Belle Dune River, NB

Kingsley, Noel Arthur
Regt # – E30156
Eaton Corner, QC

Kinnie, Ronald Murray

Regt # – E30548
Beaverbrook, NB

Knapp, William Arthur G
Regt # – E30545
Quebec City, QC

Kyryluik, Frederick
Regt # – B46174
Vita, MB

La Billois, Edgard
Regt # – E30512
Magusasha, QC

Laberge, Alfred
Regt # – E29835
Lake Edward, QC

Labrecque, Edward
Regt # – 30044
Maria East, QC

Lachance, Gerard
Regt # – E30055
Montreal, QC

Ladds, William John
Regt # – E30091
Noranda, QC

Lafferty, Harvey Reginald
Regt # – B41445
Thorold, ON

Laflamme, Thomas Paul
Regt # – E30681

Barachois, QC

Lafoe, Richard Clarence
Regt # – E29920
Richmond, QC

Lake, George Maurice
Regt # – F400964
Windsor, NB

Lalime, Jean Pierre
Regt # – E30691
Arvida, QC

Lalonde, Gordon Joseph
Regt # – C5841
Martintown, ON

Lamb, Patrick William
Regt # – E30598
Unknown

Lancaster, Russell George
Regt # – E30756
St. Christine, QC

Lancour, Walter Raymond
Regt # – C41428
Chalk River, ON

Landry, Joseph E
Regt # – E30546
Charlo, QC

Lapalme, Roland
Regt # – E30152
Bury, QC

Lapierre, Joseph Camile
Regt # – E30400
Montreal, QC

Lapointe, Archie Daniel
Regt # – E30293
Kirkland Lake, MB

Lapointe, Eugene
Regt # – E30338
Nash Creek, NB

Lapointe, Joseph Pierre
Regt # – E30651
La Tuque, QC

Lasenba, Earl
Regt # – E29932
Bury, QC

Latulippe, Maurice
Regt # – E29362
Bury, QC

Lauriault, Allan
Regt # – E30076
Maniwaki, QC

Lavoie, John
Regt # – E30362
Campbellton, NB

Law, Reginald
Regt # – E30006
Flatlands, NB

Lawlis, Philip Edwin

Regt # – E29943
Grand Cascapedia, QC

Lawrence, Bert
Regt # – E30257
Unknown

Lawrence, Joseph William E
Regt # – E30494
Barachois, NB

Laxson, Kenneth Pearly
Regt # –E40445
Danville, QC

Lebel, Valmont
Regt # – E30106
Campbellton, NB

Lebell, John
Regt # – E30105
Sault aux Recollets, QC

Leblanc, Frank
Regt # – E30616
Sherbrooke, QC

Leblanc, Jean Paul
Regt # – E30364
Unknown

Leblanc, Joseph Louis
Regt # – E30401
St. Francis d'Assise, QC

Leblanc, Joseph Napoleon
Regt # – F40741

Cape Breton, NS

Leblanc, Leandre
Regt # – E30617
Campbellton, NB

Leblanc, Leopold Paul
Regt # – E30725
Campbellton, NB

Leblanc, Louis Gerald
Regt # – E30432
Maria, QC

Lebouef, Valmont
Regt # – E30173
Campbellton, QC

Lebreton, Phillip
Regt # – E30424
Kenogame, QC

Lecouffe, Lionel Joseph
Regt # – E30621
Campbellton, QC

Lee, William James
Regt # – C40653
Oshawa, ON

Legacy, John Fidell
Regt # – E30399
Unknown

Leggo, Wesley Earl
Regt # – E30765
L'Anse a Brillant, QC

Lesieur, Beryl
Regt # – E30312
La Tuque, QC

Leslie, Franklyn George
Regt # – E30410
Magdalen Islands, QC

Lester, Wilbert E
Regt # – E30070
South Durham, QC

Levesque, Ernest Louis
Regt # – E30228
Campbellton, NB

Levitt, John
Regt # – E30069
Kingsbury, QC

Linn, James William
Regt # – C6368
Marmora, ON

Litalien, Antoine
Regt # – E30164
Mill Stream, QC

Lloyd, Ferdinand Dallen
Regt # – F77009
Doctors Cove, NS

Lloyd, Stanley Gerald
Regt # – B60896
Kingston, ON

Lockhart, Leighton Orn

Regt # – G18701
Woodstock, NB

Lockhart, Maurice E
Regt # – F40800
Greenwich, NS

Lodge, Jack
Regt # – E30037
Runnymede, QC

Long, John Richard
Regt # – G22207
Tide Head, NB

Lott, Edward Cameron
Regt # – C65568
Oshawa, ON

Lowe, Arthur Burton
Regt # – E30157
Bury, QC

Lowe, John Joseph
Regt # – E30409
Montreal, QC

Lucas, Thomas Stanley
Regt # – E29878
Belle Anse, QC

Lyons, Henry Viny
Regt # – E29994
Mann Settlement, QC

Lyons, Jack Hoseph
Regt # – G27678

Mann Settlement, QC

MacAllister, Arthur
Regt # – E30369
Nash Creek, NB

MacArthur, John Edward
Regt # – E29847
South Durham, QC

MacArthur, Murdo Neil
Regt # – E29931
Milan, QC

MacDonald, Alexander John
Regt # – E29964
Wyer's Brook, NB

MacDonald, Allison Ronald
Regt # – E29974
Wyer's Brook, NB

MacDonald, Donald
Regt # – E29973
Wyer's Brook, NB

MacDonald, Edward Leonard
Regt # – E30565
Fredrickton, NB

MacDonald, George
Regt # – E29972
Wyer's Brook, NB

MacIver, Donald
Regt # – E29954
Scotstown, QC

MacIver, Gordon Donald
Regt # – E30065
Scotstown, QC

MacIver, Harry Victor
Regt # – E30054
Scotstown, QC

MacKay, Laurie Vincent
Regt # – F50446
Truro, NS

MacKenzie, Matthew Dewey
Regt # – E30272
Ajax, ON

MacKinnon, William Wallace
Regt # – E30327
Escuminac, QC

MacKnight, Harold Wilbur
Reg#t – E30458
Campbellton, NB

MacLaughlin, Thomas
Regt # – F40988
Bass River, NS

MacLean, Charles Lewis
Regt # – E30288
Cape Breton, NS

MacLean, Ralph Angus
Regt # – E30382
Grindstone, QC

MacNaughton, Alden Lee

Regt # – E30027
Matapedia, QC

MacNaughton, Graydon D
Regt # – E30028
Matapedia, QC

MacNaughton, Joseph Robert
Regt # – E30284
Matapedia, QC

MacPherson, Clayton Keith
Regt # – C57533
Finch, ON

MacWhirter, Eldon
Regt # – E29939
New Richmond, QC

MacWhirter, William Wellington
Regt # – E30761
Hopetown, QC

Mahoney, Charles Anthony
Regt # – E30146
Flatslands, NB

Mahoney, Murray Timothy
Regt # – E30585
Sussex, NB

Main, James Stewart
Regt # – E30234
Dawsonville, NB

Major, Kenneth John
Regt # – C57531

Williamstown, ON

Major, Wilson
Regt # – E30696
Hopetown, QC

Malboeuf, Auguste
Regt # – E30194
Kingsbury, QC

Malley, Joseph Morris
Regt # – E30179
Glencoe, NB

Maloney, Eddie Joseph
Regt # – E29882
Barachois, QC

Maloney, Eric
Regt # – E29890
Douglastown, QC

Maloof, Steve Joseph
Regt # – E30287
Noranda, QC

Maloof, Wilfred Joseph
Regt # – E30297
Noranda, QC

Manclark, William
   Fatheringham
Regt # – B68237
Toronto, ON

Mann, Cecil Marcillus
Regt # – E30449

Runnymede, QC

Mann, Glenford Finley
Regt # – E30009
Matapedia, QC

Mann, James Burnett
Regt # – E30127
Oak Bay Mills, QC

Mann, Maxwell Arthur
Regt # – E30022
Upsalquitch, NB

Mann, Richard
Regt # – E29995
Flatlands, NB

Mann, Weston
Regt # – E29998
Mann Settlement, QC

Marcoux, Gerard
Regt # – E30246
Sawerville, QC

Marshall, Howard Thomas
Regt # – C65148
Lindsay, ON

Marsolais, Henry Joseph
Regt # – C57537
Cornwall, ON

Marston, Jeffery Charles
Regt # – C65584
Oshawa, ON

Martin, Douglas John
Regt # – E30237
Campbellton, NB

Martin, Henry
Regt # – E30760
Bury, QC

Martin, John Keith Lionel
Regt # – E29802
Montreal, QC

Martin, Paul
Regt # – E30167
Resigouche, QC

Mason, Frederick Charles
Regt # – B60573
Oshawa, ON

Mason, Frederick James
Regt # – B68240
Toronto, ON

Masson, Gustave Adelard
Regt # – E30089
Espanola, ON

Matheson, Harold
Regt # – E29927
Compton, QC

Mayhew, Richie James
Regt # – E30189
Lac Megantic, QC

Maynes, Harold Everett

Regt # – C5865
Point Anne, ON

Mazerolle, Emile
Regt # – E30555
Peters Mill, NB

McAra, William Roger
Regt # – E30124
Unknown

McArthur, Frederick Arthur
Regt # – C65346
Toronto, ON

McBeath, Earl Eldridge
Regt # – G17885
Ripples, NB

McCarron, Thomas Patrick
Regt # – E30385
Benjamin River, NB

McColm, Frank Howard
Regt # – E30349
New Carlisle, QC

McColm, Murray Ralph
Regt # – E30714
Verdun, QC

McCorkell, Hector Gordon
Regt # – C65573
Toronto, ON

McDavid, Clifford Edward
Regt # – E30447

Matapedia, QC

McDavid, John Jeffrey
Regt # – E30454
Matapedia, QC

McDonald, Milton Douglas
Regt # – E30184
Lac Megantic, QC

McDonald, Robert Lee
Regt # – E30165
St. Alexis, QC

McEachern, John Aloysious
Regt # – F54969
Sydney, NS

McFawn, Lewis Robert
Regt # – G18052
Fredericton, NB

McGinn, Robert Eugene
Regt # – E30562
Fredericton, NB

McGrath, Jean
Regt # – E30702
Richardville, NB

McGrath, William Joseph
Regt # – E30283
McGrath Cove, NS

McGregor, Herman Malcolm
Regt # – C65019
Lindsay, ON

McGuire, Ralph Eldred
Regt # – E30568
Port Daniel West, QC

McIntyre, George Joseph
Regt # – E30528
Charlot Station, NB

McIsaac, Joseph Jamieson
Regt # – E30672
Inverness, NS

McKay, Andrew John
Regt # – C40618
Lindsay, ON

McKay, John
Regt # – E30629
Nash Creek, NB

McKee, Charles Hugh
Regt # – B75058
Chapleau, ON

McKenna, Charles Stephen
Regt # – B64630
Toronto, ON

McKinley, Sterling
Regt # – E29981
Broadlands, QC

McLaughlin, Robert
Regt # – E30625
Campbellton, NB

McLean, John James

Regt # – B68216
Toronto, ON

McLeod, Roderick
Regt # – B41357
Powell River BC

McTeer, William Eric
Regt # – B41362
Hamilton, ON

McWhirter, John
Regt # – E29945
New Richmond, QC

Meade, Ernest Joseph
Regt # – E30375
Jacquet River, NB

Medhurst, George
Regt # – C65164
Cobourg, ON

Merchie, Albert
Regt # – E30627
Unknown

Meredith, Clifford
Regt # – 29955
New Richmond, QC

Meredith, Earl John
Regt # – E29993
New Richmond, QC

Metallic, Patrick
Regt # – E30097

Resigouche, QC

Methot, Frank
Regt # – E29862
Resigouche, QC

Miller, Ernest James
Regt # – E30373
Jacquet River, NB

Miller, Joseph Howard
Regt # – E30192
Lac Megantic, QC

Mills, Alfred R
Regt # – E30085
Melbourne, QC

Mohan, James Werin
Regt # – B49394
Midland, ON

Moir, Andrew Muir
Regt # – C65625
Lindsay, ON

Moles, William David
Regt # – A33101
Wiarton, ON

Moore, Claude
Regt # – E29985
New Richmond, QC

Moore, Reginald Harry
Regt # – C65315
Campbellford, ON

Moore, Walter Leslie
Regt # – F40761
Kentville, NS

Moores, Lawson James
Regt # – E30015
Matapedia, QC

Mortimer, James Lake
Regt # – B41307
Dundalk, ON

Mossman, Earl Gilbert
Regt # – F40841
Saint John, NB

Muir, Kenneth
Regt # – E29868
Windsor Mills, QC

Mulherin, Lawrence Percival
Regt # – C48469
Grand Falls, NB

Mullin, Elmer Owen
Regt # – E30663
Brassett, QC

Murchie, Albert Borden
Regt # – E30624
Nash Creek, NB

Murphy, Claud Patrick
Regt # – E30606
Halifax, NS

Murphy, Leo

Regt # – E30638
New Richmond, QC

Murphy, Reynald
Regt # – E30639
New Richmond, QC

Murray, George Wesley
Regt # – A23153
Walled Lake, MC, USA

Murray, Gordon M
Regt # – E29975
Flatlands, NB

Murray, Mathew William
Regt # – C6387
Oshawa, ON

Murray, Raymond
Regt # – E29863
Chandler, QC

Myers, Gerald Guy
Regt # – F35180
Ostrea Lake, NS

Nellis, Leo Francis
Regt # – E30239
Flatlands, NB

Newell, Lorne Robert
Regt # – E30303
Lisgar, QC

Nicol, Ralph
Regt # – E30098

Sellarsville, QC

Nicholson, Clifford Murray
Regt # – E30607
Milan, QC

Nicholson, William
Regt # – B40683
Toronto, ON

Noble, Russell G
Regt # – E30196
Melbourne, QC

Noel, William Henry
Regt # – E30504
Durham Centre, NB

Normand, Andre
Regt # – E30686
D'Aiguillon, QC

Noseworthy, Percy
Regt # – E30733
St. John's, NL

Oakley, Raymond Joseph
Regt # – E30552
Midland, ON

O'Leary, Lloyd William
Regt # – E30476
Perce, QC

Olscamp, Robert
Regt # – E30119
Cross Point, QC

Olson, Eric Lynn
Regt # – E29933
Bury, QC

Olsson, Carl Barton
Regt # – E30502
Point Navarrl, QC

Ouellet, Marcel
Regt # – E29821
Malane, QC

Pappas, William Stephen
Regt # – E30767
Cleveland, OH, USA

Parenteau, Joseph Robert
Regt # – E29918
Sherbrooke, QC

Passmore, Francis Paul
Regt # – B68207
Allandale, ON

Patrick, Leonard
Regt # – E30542
Melbourne, QC

Patterson, James Richard
Regt # – E30580
Sussex, NB

Pattingale, Jame Reuben
Regt # – F34683
Maplewood, NS

Pellitier, Algee A

Regt # – G17301
Edmundston, NB

Pelletier, Gerard Joseph
Regt # – E30315
Rouyn, QC

Pentland, Gerard Patrick
Regt # – E30214
Escundunac, QC

Perreault, Isidore
Regt # – E29696
Fontenelle, QC

Pete, Leo
Regt # – E30560
Culligan, NB

Pidgeon, Joseph Arthur Eugene
Regt # – E30487
Perce, QC

Pifher, Arthur Kenneth
Regt # – B43098
Paris, ON

Pineault, Armand
Regt # – E30372
Matapedia, QC

Pitre, Robert
Regt # – E30111
La Giraudois, QC

Poag, Russell Vernon
Regt # – B38160

Caledonia, ON

Poirier, Joseph Patrick
Regt # – E30271
Noranda, QC

Poirier, Levis Joseph
Regt # – E30366
Eel River Crossing, NB

Pollock, Allison
Regt # – E30460
Glen Levit, NB

Pollock, Coleman
Regt # – E30342
Dawsonville, NB

Pollock, Duncan Malcolm
Regt # – E30224
Glen Levit, NB

Pollock, Frederick William
Regt # – E30558
Norton, NB

Pollock, Kirk Allan
Regt # – E30467
Glen Levit, NB

Pollock, Simon Fraser
Regt # – E30330
Campbellton, NB

Pomeroy, George Robert
Regt # – C65270
Castleton, ON

Porter, Arnold James
Regt # – E30225
Campbellton, NB

Porterfield, Leo Edward
Regt # – E30093
Noranda, QC

Post, John Russell
Regt # – G18468
Aroostock, NB

Potts, William George
Regt # – C57528
Port Hope, ON

Powers, Vincent
Regt # – E30720
Campbellton, NB

Pratt, Porter
Regt # – E30019
Matapedia, QC

Provencher, Jules
Regt # - E30421
New Richmond, QC

Pryce, Arnold
Regt # – E29852
Sherbrooke, QC

Quirion, Raymond
Regt # – E30486
Perce, QC

Rame, Charles Edward

Regt # – B46249
Toronto, ON

Ramier, Goldie George
Regt # – E30254
Port Daniel West, QC

Randall, Arthur Edward
Regt # – B40750
Port Colbourne, ON

Rattie, Alexander
Regt # – E30140
Cross Point, QC

Rattie, Lawrence
Regt # – E30166
Mann Settlement, QC

Ray, Irvin Kirwin
Regt # – F29946
St. Marys River, NS

Rees, Douglas Bartlett
Regt # – E30729
St. John's, NL

Reid, Colin
Regt # – E30484
Quebec City, QC

Reid, Douglas Joseph
Regt # – E30483
Quebec City, QC

Reid, Lloyd George
Regt # – C41424

Almonte, ON

Richard, Joseph Francois Leo
Regt # – E30543
Quebec City, QC

Rideout, William John
Regt # – G18211
Bath, NB

Riley, James Clayton
Regt # – B41458
Unknown

Roberts, Arthur Gosse
Regt # – E306855
Little Gaspe, QC

Robertson, Francis
Regt # – E30263
Maria East, QC

Robertson, Louis
Regt # – E29942
New Richmond, QC

Robertson, Oscar
Regt # – E29946
New Richmond, QC

Robinson, Clifford
Regt # – E29962
Windsor Mills, QC

Roblee, Lloyd Logan
Regt # – F40323
Springhill, NS

Rooney, Leonard
Regt # – E29880
Douglastown, QC

Ross, Cyril Matthew
Regt # – E30444
Hopetown, QC

Ross, Eric Arnold
Regt # – E29953
New Richmond, QC

Ross, Lawrence Alexander
Regt # – E29339
Bury, QC

Ross, Leo Joseph
Regt # – E29341
Unknown

Ross, Raymond
Regt # – E29343
Bury, QC

Roussel, John R
Regt # – E30316
Bathurst, NB

Rowen, Alfred Ernest
Regt # – B68208
Toronto, ON

Rowland, Roney
Regt # – A3625
Durham, NS

Roy, Albert

Regt # – E38179
Atholville, NB

Roy, Bertram Andrew
Regt # – E30452
Jacquet, NB

Royer, James Cecil
Regt # – E30240
Bury, QC

Russell, Albert James
Regt # – E22957
Quebec City, QC

Russell, John David
Regt # – F40198
Springhill, NS

Salter, Henry
Regt # – E30047
Cookshire, QC

Sandford, Matthew James
Regt # – B64169
Toronto, ON

Sarty, Perry
Regt # – F40751
Mersey Point, NS

Savoy, Edward Joseph
Regt # – G32318
Saint John, NB

Schofield, Reginald James
Regt # – C65117

Wilberforce, ON

Schrage, David M
Regt # –B38365
Unknown

Scobie, Garnet
Regt # – C41390
Haley's Station, ON

Serroul, Vincent Russel
Regt # – F40361
Little Bras D'Or, NS

Shalala, John Alexander
Regt # – E30441
Campbellton, NB

Shane, Samuel
Regt # – E29870
Cornwall, ON

Shaw, George Arthur
Regt # – E30020
Kenogami, QC

Sheldon, Bertram
Regt # – B64673
Toronto, ON

Siddall, Hilton Albert
Regt # – G18280
Sackville, NB

Simmons, Gordon
Regt # – E30682
South Bathurst, NB

Sirois, Guy
Regt # – E30186
Edmundson, NB

Skelton, Sydney
Regt # – B63742
Toronto, ON

Smith, Edward Albert
Regt # – E30278
Trenholmville, QC

Smith, Harold Alexander
Regt # – B40918
St. Catherines, ON

Smith, John Hamilton
Regt # – E30121
Kenogami, QC

Smith, Lawrence
Regt # – E30279
Trenholmville, QC

Smith, Norman Alfred
Regt # – C63078
Clayton, ON

Smith, Raymond Angus
Regt # – E29841
Scotstown, QC

Smith, Robert Archibald
Regt # – G27295
Glen Levit, NB

Smith, Wilfred Duncan

Regt # – E30376
Glen Levit, NB

Smith, William John
Regt # – E30435
Chatham, NB

Snear, Thomas W
Regt # – E30461
Unknown

Sneddon, Jack Gerald
Regt # – B68222
Toronto, ON

Snell, Felix Maxwell
Regt # – C57527
Port Hope, ON

Snively, John Thomas
Regt # – A22721
Kingsville, ON

Sommerville, Stanley S
Regt # – E30772
Quebec City, QC

Soper, George Arthur
Regt # – B45667
Toronto, ON

Southworth, Donald Frederick
Regt # – C65332
Campbellford, ON

Spencley, Walter Joseph
Regt # – B72966

Peterborough, ON

Splude, George Raymond
Regt # – E30339
Moncton, NB

St. Croix, John Edwin
Regt # – E30492
Barachois, QC

St. John, Ralph Elwood
Regt # – B75066
Toronto, ON

St. Onge, John
Regt # – E29992
GE Maria East, QC

Steele, Randolph David
Regt # – E1145
Grand Cascapedia, QC

Steeves, George
Regt # – E30619
Nash Creek, NB

Stepanchuk, Nick
Regt # – B40630
Port Colborne, ON

Stevens, Clarence George
Regt # – E30497
Danville, QC

Street, Sydney Charles
Regt # – B63830
Toronto, ON

Stroud, John Raymond
Regt # – B76772
Toronto, ON

Suits, William Roger
Regt # – A23080
Dowanaic, MI, USA

Sullivan, Fergus
Regt # – E30253
Shigawake East, QC

Sullivan, Robert Thomas
Regt # – E30174
Blackland, NB

Sunstrum, Gerald
Regt # – B68309
Niagara Falls, ON

Surette, Henry Andrew
Regt # – F40743
Port Bickerton, NB

Swanson, Kurt S.W.
Regt # – M61729
Unknown

Sweet, Royce Charles
Regt # – E30622
West Bathurst, NB

Sweetman, Herbert F
Regt # – E30259
Bonaventure, QC

Syvret, David

Regt # – E29879
Belle Anse, QC

Tainsh, William George
Regt # – C65118
Lindsay, ON

Tapp, Harry Joachim
Regt # – E29866
Barachois, QC

Taylor, Reginald Samuel
Regt # – E29853
East Kildonan, MB

Taylor, Robert William
Regt # – A22374
Windsor, ON

Tennier, Joseph Arthur
Regt # – E30752
Hopetown, QC

Tetreault, Adrien
Regt # – E30455
South Durham, QC

Theriault, Oswald
Regt # – E30030
Asbestos, QC

Thirlwell, Frederick
Regt # – B38367
Alliston, ON

Thompson, Bernard M
Regt # – E30541

Glen Levit, NB

Thompson, Clarence Walton
Regt # – C65460
Port Hope, ON

Thompson, John Alexander
Regt # – G22778
Dawsonville, NB

Thompson, Morton George
    Clinton
Regt # – E30427
Glen Levit, NB

Thompson, Raymond Michael
Regt # – E30226
Campbellton, NB

Thompson, Renwick Lynn
Regt # – E30248
Compton, QC

Thompson, Thomas Edward
Regt # – G18342
Richibucto, NB

Thompson, Wendell Godfrey
Regt # – E30348
Nash Creek, NB

Tibbitts, Clifford Felix
Regt # – E29858
Waterloo, QC

Todd, John Byng
Regt # – B40690

Stamford Centre, ON

Trahan, Albert
Regt # – E30305
South Durham, QC

Tremblay, Raoul
Regt # – E30664
Prevel, QC

Trites, Leverette John
Regt # – G18587
Moncton, NB

Tuppert, William Gerald Joseph
Regt # – E22893
Quebec City, QC

Turcotte, Arthur Dominick
Regt # – C5895
Arnprior, ON

Tyler, Stanley
Regt # – E30496
Campbellton, NB

Valcourt, Leo
Regt # – E30308
Scotstown, QC

Vanclief, Donald John
Regt # – C5898
Consecon, ON

Varley, John Leslie
Regt # – B24237
Toronto, ON

Vigneault, Laureat
Regt # – F41026
Boisville, QC

Vincent, Charles
Regt # – E22897
Quebec City, QC

Vincent, Kenneth Stanley
Regt # – E30462
Campbellton, NB

Vincent, Robert Leslie
Regt # – E30518
River Charlo, NB

Wall, Frederick Leonard
Regt # – E30433
Gaspe, QC

Wallace, Herbert A
Regt # – E30195
Kingsbury, QC

Wallace, James Austin
Regt # – F29945
Kentville, NS

Walsh, James Edward
Regt # – G18634
Moncton, NB

Walsh, Joseph Edward
Regt # – E30582
Penobsquis, NB

Walton, Jack
Regt # – C65283

Toronto, ON

Ward, Howard Guy
Regt # – E30159
Bury, QC

Wardell, Thomas David
Regt # – E30634
St. John's NL

Waterhouse, William Edmond
Regt # – E30759
Melbourne, QC

Watters, Ira Gordon
Regt # – E30556
Apohaqui, NB

Watts, Eric George
Regt # – E30073
Unknown

Weaver, Percy Thomas
Regt # – B38362
Haliburton, ON

Webb, James Christopher
Regt # – E30576
Norton, NB

Webb, John Frederick
Regt # – E30579
Norton, NB

Wellman, David
Regt # – C5898
Bonarlaw, ON

Welsh, Allen Benjamin
Regt # – E30395
Magdalen Islands, QC

Welsh, Delbert William Louis
Regt # – E30384
Magdalen Islands, QC

Welsh, Ernest Edwin
Regt # – E30397
Magdalen Islands, QC

Welsh, Melvin Burton
Regt # – E30396
Magdalen Islands, QC

Whalen, Joseph Michael
Regt # – C65092
Kirkfield, ON

Wheeler, Robert Ritchie
Regt # – E30448
Runnymede, QC

Wilbur, Angus Frank
Regt # – E30489
South Bathurst, NB

Wilbur, Clarence Joseph G
Regt # – E30485
South Bathurst, NB

Willett, Byron Joseph
Regt # – E30010
Grand Cascapedia, QC

Willett, Frederick

Regt # – E30141
Cross Point, QC

Willett, Isaac Alan
Regt # – E30374
Campbellton, NB

Willett, Percy J
Regt # – E29991
Bonaventure, QC

Willey, Ivan Emmerson
Regt # – E30306
Danville, QC

Williams, John Arthur
Regt # – A23182
Alpena, MI, USA

Wills, John Harry
Regt # – B68239
Mount Dennis, ON

Wilmot, Percy Horace
Regt # – B40839
St. Catharines, ON

Wilson, Lawrence Joseph
Regt # – B38366
Baind, ON

Wing, Peter
Regt # – B317
Unknown

Wood, Donald Gordon
Regt # – E30176

Frontenac County, QC

Woodman, Bertram C
Regt # – E29947
Campbellton, NB

Woodrich, Russell Lincoln
Regt # – A23001
East Windsor, ON

Wurm, Gilbert Albert
Regt # – C6352
Arnprior, ON

Wyrwas, Frederick Arnold
Regt # – E30138
Inverness, NS

Young, Walter Rintoul
Regt # – B38369
Merriton, ON

Youngs, Clarence Franklin
Regt # – A37959
Wallaceburg, ON

Zaidman, Frederick
Regt # – B40578
Winnipeg, MB

Courtesy of the Hong
  Kong Veterans'
  Commemorative
  Association

Appendix C
List of "C" Force Killed or Missing in Action

Brigade

Col. P. Hennessy, age 56
Died of wounds, 1941/12/20
Sai Wan Cemetary, Grave #VIII. C.4

Brig. J.K. Lawson, age 54
Wong Nei Chong Gap, believed killed
    1941/12/19
Sai Wan Cemetary, Grave #VIII C.27

Maj. C.A. Lyndon, age nk
Wong Nei Chong Gap, 1941/12/20
Sai Wan Memorial, Column 23

Corps of Military Staff Clerks

Sgt. M.F. Black, age nk
Wong Nei Chong Gap, 1941/12/19
Sai Wan Cemetary, Grave #VIII A.11

Sgt. C.L. Jewitt, age nk
Wong Nei Chong Gap, 1941/12/19
Sai Wan Memorial, Column 27

Sgt. W.E. Phillips, age nk
Wong Nei Chong Gap, 1941/12/19
Sai Wan Memorial, Column 28

Royal Canadian Army Pay Corps

Capt. R.M.B. Davies, age 39
At Mount Austin Barracks by concussion from
    shellfire, 1941/12/20
Sai Wan Cemetary, Grave #VIII B. 8

Royal Canadian Army Service Corps

Pte. M. Berger, age 35
The Ridge, 1941/12/19
Sai Wan Memorial, Column 28

Capt. O.S. Hickey, age 32
Stanley massacre, killed trying to protect the
    nurses, 1941/12/25
Sai Wan Memorial, Column 27

Pte. A. Jackson, age 42
The Ridge, 1941/12/19
Sai Wan Memorial, Column 27

Pte. D.S. Melville, age 39
Died in hospital, wounded at Wan Chai Gap
    driving Colonel Hennesy to Wong Nei
    Chong Gap, 1941/12/19
Stanley Military Cemetary, 6. B. Coll. Grave
    3-14

Pte. A. Newsome, age nk
Wong Nei Chong Gap, 1941/12/19
Sai Wan Memorial, Column 28

Royal Canadian Corps of Signals

Sgm. R. Damant, age 21
Wan Chai Gap, 1941/12/19
Stanley Military Cemetary, 6. B. Coll. Grave
        12-19

Sgm. J.L.F. Farley, age 21
Died in hospital of wounds, 1941/12/22
Stanley Military Cemetary, 6. B. Coll. Grave
        1-12

Sgm. H. Greenberg, age nk
Wan Chai, 1941/12/19
Stanley Military Cemetary, 6. B. Coll. Grave
        12-19

Sgm. J.E. Horvath, age 21
Wan Chai Gap, died of wounds (?), 1942/01/01
Sai Wan Memorial, Column 27

Cpl. C.J. Sharp, age 26
Wan Chai, 1941/12/23
Stanley Military Cemetary, 6. B. Coll. Grave
        12-19

Sgm. E.R. Thomas, age nk
Wong Nei Chong Gap, dispatch driver killed at,
        1941/12/19
Sai Wan Memorial, Column 27

Royal Canadian Ordnance Corps

Cpl. G.G. Desroches, age nk
The Ridge, 1941/12/19
Sai Wan Memorial, Column 26

SSgt. G. Jackman, age 21
The Ridge, 1941/12/24
Sai Wan Memorial, Column 27

Pte. F.C. McGuire, age 24
The Ridge, 1941/12/19
Sai Wan Memorial, Column 28

The Royal Rifles of Canada

Rfm. J.A. Acorn, age nk
Location of battle death nk, 1941/12/23
Sai Wan Memorial, Column 24

Rfm. J.M. Acorn, age 28
Location of battle death nk, 1941/12/23
Sai Wan Memorial, Column 24

Rfm. B.H. Adams, age nk
Died of wounds, 1941/12/25
Sai Wan Cemetery, Grave #VIII A. 2

Rfm. L. Allen, age nk
Eucliffe, 1941/12/23
Sai Wan Memorial, Column 24

Rfm. A.L. Andrews, age 30
Repulse Bay Hotel, 1941/12/23
Sai Wan Memorial, Column 24

Rfm. J. Arseneau, age nk
Believed 41 Dec 15, burial at Stanley Cemetery,
        1941/12/21
Sai Wan Memorial, Column 24

Rfm. P. Atwood, age 19
Repulse Bay, 1941/12/23

Sai Wan Memorial, Column 24

Rfm. J.V. Baker, age 18
Location of battle death nk, 1941/12/25
Stanley Military Cemetery, 5. C. Coll. Grave
    4-20

Rfm. C.G. Barnett, age 18
Palm Villa, 1941/12/21
Sai Wan Memorial, Column 24

Rfm. E. Bate, age nk
Stanley Mound, 1941/12/22
Sai Wan Memorial, Column 23

Rfm. R.R. Beacroft, age 18
Lye Mun, 1941/12/19
Sai Wan Memorial, Column 24

Sgt. L.A. Beattie, age 20
Location of battle death nk, 1941/12/23
Sai Wan Memorial, Column 23

Rfm. E. Bertin, age 28
St. Stephen's College, died of wounds,
    1941/12/25
Sai Wan Memorial, Column 24

Rfm. W. Best, age 27
Repulse Bay, 1941/12/23
Sai Wan Memorial, Column 24

Rfm. V.E. Boudreau, age 23
Stanley Mound, 1941/12/26
Sai Wan Memorial, Column 24

Rfm. N. Bouley, age nk

Stanley View, 1941/12/23
Sai Wan Memorial, Column 24

Rfm. R. Briand, age 29
Repulse Bay, 1941/12/23
Sai Wan Memorial, Column 24

Rfm. H. Bujold, age nk
Repulse Bay, 1941/12/23
Sai Wan Memorial, Column 24

Rfm. W.J. Burgess, age 22
Stanley Mound, 1941/12/26
Sai Wan Memorial, Column 24

Rfm. G. Calder, age nk
Tai Tam Gap, 1941/12/19
Sai Wan Memorial, Column 24

Rfm. R.K. Chalmers, age 21
Wong Nei Chong Gap, 1941/12/26
Sai Wan Memorial, Column 24

Rfm. O.J. Chatterton, age 23
Location of battle death nk, 1941/12/23
Sai Wan Cemetery, Grave #VIII. A. 21

Cpl. J.A. Coleman, age 26
Bowen Road Hospital died of wounds,
    1942/02/18
Stanley Military Cemetery, 6. A. Coll. Grave
    1-12

Cpl. A.R. Collins, age 18
Stone Hill, 1941/12/23
Sai Wan Memorial, Column 23

Rfm. F. Cormier, age 34
Stanley Fort, 1941/12/25
Stanley Military Cemetery, 5. A. Coll. Grave
    4-20

Rfm. P.G. Crosman, age nk
Location of battle death nk
Sai Wan Memorial, Column 23

Sgt. J.G. Cuzner, age nk
Lye Mun, murdered by Japanese at C Coy HQ,
    1941/12/19
Sai Wan Memorial, Column 23

Rfm. E. Cyr, age 21
Location of battle death nk, 1941/12/19
Sai Wan Cemetery, Grave #VIII. B. 5

Rfm. J. Delaney, age 23
Notting Hill, 1941/12/21
Sai Wan Memorial, Column 24

Rfm. M. Delaney, age nk
Died of wounds, 1942/01/04
Sai Wan Memorial, Column 24

Rfm. A.A. Dixon, age 36
St. Stephen's Hospital, 1941/12/26
Sai Wan Memorial, Column 24

Rfm. A. Doran, age nk
Red Hill, 1941/12/26
Sai Wan Memorial, Column 24

Rfm. E. Doucet, age 18
Location of battle death nk, 1941/12/23
Sai Wan Memorial, Column 24

Rfm. J.L. Doyle, age nk
Spanish House between Repulse Bay and
    Deepwater Bays, 1941/12/22
Sai Wan Memorial, Column 24

Rfm. E.G. Dupont, age 18
Stanley Prison, 1941/12/24
Sai Wan Cemetery, Grave #IX. E. 1

Rfm. J.E. Evans, age nk
Died of wounds, 1941/12/26
Sai Wan Cemetery, Grave #VIII. B. 11

LCpl. W. Fallow, age nk
St. Stephen's Hospital, 1941/12/25
Sai Wan Memorial, Column 23

Rfm. J.F. Firlotte, age 22
Location of battle death nk, 1941/12/23
Sai Wan Memorial, Column 24

Cpl. J.J. Fitzpatrick, age nk
Killed by shell, 1941/12/22
Sai Wan Memorial, Column 23

Rfm. D.W. Forsyth, age 18
Died of wounds, 1941/12/25
Stanley Military Cemetery, 5. C. Coll. Grave
    4-20

Liet. W.S. Fry, age 34
Killed Red Hill with Bompas of HKSRA,
    1941/12/21
Sai Wan Memorial, Column 23

Rfm. B.J. Gallant, age nk
Stanley Mound, 1941/12/22

Sai Wan Memorial, Column 24

Rfm. C. Gallant, age 18
Repulse Bay, 1941/12/22
Sai Wan Memorial, Column 24

Rfm. M. Gammack, age 41
Stanley View, 1941/12/22
Sai Wan Memorial, Column 24

Sgt. Gander, age nk
Location of battle death nk, 1941/12/19
No military grave or memorial

Rfm. O. Geraghty, age nk
Stone Hill, 1941/12/23
Sai Wan Memorial, Column 23

Rfm. W.J. Grieves, age 21
Repulse Bay Hotel, 1941/12/20
Sai Wan Memorial, Column 24

Rfm. G. Halley, age nk
Mount Parker, 1941/12/19
Sai Wan Memorial, Column 24

LCpl. A.C. Harrison, age 19
Salesian Massacre, murdered at the, 1941/12/19
Sai Wan Memorial, Column 23

LCpl. E.E. Harrison, age nk
Mount Parker, 1941/12/19
Sai Wan Memorial, Column 23

Rfm. E.J. Henderson, age 21
St. Stephen's Hospital, murdered, 1941/12/25
Sai Wan Memorial, Column 24

Rfm. C.G. Hickey, age nk
Lye Mun, 1941/12/19
Sai Wan Cemetery, Grave #VIII. C. 5

Rfm. L.R. Hopgood, age 19
Sai Wan, 1941/12/19
Sai Wan Cemetery, Grave #VIII. C. 9

Sgt. H.B. Hughes, age 31
Mount Parker, 1941/12/19
Sai Wan Memorial, Column 23

Rfm. H. Hunchuck, age nk
Bungalow C, 1941/12/25
Stanley Military Cemetery, 1. B. Coll. Grave 2-9

Rfm. B. Irvine, age nk
Stanley Village, 1941/12/25
Sai Wan Memorial, Column 24

Rfm. C. Irvine, age 18
Stanley, 1941/12/25
Sai Wan Memorial, Column 24

Rfm. G. Irvine, age nk
Killed same shell that wounded Capt Gavey, 41
    Dec 18, 1941/12/19
Sai Wan Memorial, Column 25

Rfm. R.D. Jackson, age 21
Stone Hill, 1941/12/23
Sai Wan Cemetery, Grave #VIII. C.16

Rfm. D. Jacques, age nk
Repulse Bay, 1941/12/23
Sai Wan Memorial, Column 25

Rfm. E.R. Keating, age nk
Stanley Mound, 1941/12/22
Sai Wan Memorial, Column 25

Rfm. R.M. Kinnie, age 19
Location of battle death nk, 1941/12/25
Stanley Military Cemetery, 5. C. Coll. Grave
    4-20

Rfm. H.R. Lafferty, age 20
Location of battle death nk, 1941/12/25
Sai Wan Cemetery, Grave #VIII. C.20

Rfm. J.P. LaPointe, age nk
Location of battle death nk, 1941/12/23
Sai Wan Memorial, Column 25

Cpl. L.R. Latimer, age nk
Palm Villa, killed putting Vickers Gun into
    action, 1941/12/22
Sai Wan Cemetery, Grave #VIII. C.25

Rfm. V. Lebel, age 30
Repulse Bay, 1941/12/23
Sai Wan Memorial, Column 25

Rfm. J.W. Linn, age nk
West Palm Villa, 1941/12/23
Sai Wan Memorial, Column 25

LCpl. O.L. Little, age 27
Died of wounds, 1941/12/29
Sai Wan Cemetery, Grave #VIII. D.5

Rfm. J.R. Long, age nk
Chung Hom Yok, 1941/12/26
Sai Wan Memorial, Column 25

Rfm. J.J. Lyons, age 20
St. Stephen's College, Stanley Village, killed by
    shell, 1941/12/25
Sai Wan Memorial, Column 23

Lieut. F.N. Lyster, age nk
Stanley Mound, 1941/12/24
Sai Wan Memorial, Column 23

Rfm. C.L. MacLean, age 25
Stanley Village, 1941/12/25
Sai Wan Memorial, Column 25

Rfm. M.T. Mahoney, age nk
Stanley Village, 1941/12/26
Sai Wan Memorial, Column 25

Rfm. J.S. Main, age nk
St. Stephen's College, died of wounds,
    1941/12/26
Sai Wan Memorial, Column 25

Rfm. K.J. Major, age 24
Nottinghill, 1941/12/21
Sai Wan Memorial, Column 25

Rfm. W. Major, age 21
Stanley, 1941/12/25
Sai Wan Memorial, Column 25

Rfm. J.B. Mann, age 32
Stanley Village, 1941/12/25
Sai Wan Memorial, Column 25

Cpl. G.H. Martel, age nk
Spanish House between Repulse and
    Deepwater Bays, 1941/12/23

Sai Wan Memorial, Column 23

Rfm. P. Martin, age 20
Location of battle death nk, 1941/12/23
Sai Wan Memorial, Column 25

Cpl. W. McClellan, age 32
Stanley Village, 1941/12/25
Sai Wan Memorial, Column 23

Rfm. W.J. McGrath, age 21
Stanley Mound, 1941/12/23
Sai Wan Memorial, Column 25

Rfm. R.E. McGuire, age nk
Location of battle death nk, 1941/12/25
Sai Wan Cemetery, Grave #VIII. D. 22

Rfm. J.J. McIsaac, age nk
Repulse Bay Hotel, 1941/12/23
Sai Wan Memorial, Column 25

Rfm. J. McKay, age 21
St. Stephen's College, murdered at, 1941/12/25
Sai Wan Memorial, Column 25

Sgt. L.R. McNab, age 23
Junction of Repulse Bay and Island Road,
     1941/12/22
Sai Wan Memorial, Column 23

Cpl. G.W. McCrae, age nk
Mount Parker, 1941/12/19
Sai Wan Memorial, Column 23

Rfm. J. McWhirter, age nk
Repulse Bay Hotel, 1941/12/23

Sai Wan Memorial, Column 25

LCpl. E. Meredith, age 20
Repulse Bay, 1941/12/23
Sai Wan Memorial, Column 23

Rfm. J.W. Mohan, age 24
Repulse Bay hotel, 1941/41/24
Sai Wan Memorial, Column 23

Rfm. A.R. Moir, age nk
Fort Stanley, 1941/12/25
Stanley Military Cemetery, 5. C. Coll. Grave 4-20

Rfm. C. Moore, age nk
Location of battle death nk, 1941/12/26
Sai Wan Memorial, Column 25

Rfm. W.L. Moore, age nk
Repulse Bay, 1941/12/23
Sai Wan Memorial, Column 25

Rfm. C.P. Murphy, age 18
Location of battle death nk, 1941/12/26
Sai Wan Memorial, Column 26

Rfm. R. Murphy, age nk
Location of battle death nk, 1941/12/21
Sai Wan Memorial, Column 26

Rfm. L.F. Nellis, age nk
Stanley Village, 1941/12/25
Sai Wan Memorial, Column 26

Rfm. L.R. Newell, age nk
Stanley Mound, 1941/12/22
Sai Wan Memorial, Column 26

Rfm. W.H. Noel, age 19
Stanley Mound, 1941/12/22
Sai Wan Memorial, Column 26

Rfm. P. Noseworthy, age nk
St. Stephen's College, killed near, 1941/12/25
Sai Wan Memorial, Column 26

Rfm. R.J. Oakley, age 20
Salesian Massacre, murdered at the,
    1941/12/19
Sai Wan Memorial, Column 26

Rfm. R.V. Poag, age 31
Bungalow C, 1941/12/25
Stanley Military Cemetery, 1. C. Coll. Grave
    13-17

Rfm. D.M. Pollock, age nk
Stanley Mound, 1941/12/22
Sai Wan Memorial, Column 26

Rfm. F.W. Pollock, age 24
Wong Nei Chong Gap, 1941/12/25
Sai Wan Memorial, Column 26

Rfm. W.G. Potts, age 20
Location of battle death nk, 1941/12/20
Sai Wan Memorial, Column 26

Rfm. P. Pratt, age 18
Lye Mun, 1941/12/23
Sai Wan Memorial, Column 26

Rfm. A. Rattie, age 20
Eucliffe, murdered at, 1941/12/20
Sai Wan Cemetery, Grave #VIII. E. 13

Rfm. C. Reid, age 18
Overbays House, last seen wound in blazing,
    1941/12/23
Sai Wan Memorial, Column 26

Rfm. O. Robertson, age 28
Repulse Bay, 1941/12/23
Sai Wan Memorial, Column 26

Rfm. L. Rooney, age nk
Stanley Mound, 1941/12/22
Sai Wan Memorial, Column 26

Lieut. J.F. Ross, age nk
Stanley Mound, 1941/12/22
Sai Wan Memorial, Column 23

LCpl. A.G.A. Sannes, age nk
Sugar Loaf Hill, recapturing the Vickers gun,
    1941/12/22
Sai Wan Cemetery, Grave #VIII. E. 22

Rfm. G. Scobie, age 23
Location of battle death nk, 1941/12/22
Sai Wan Memorial, Column 24

Lieut. A.B. Scott, age nk
Stanley Mound, Stanley View?, 1941/12/24
Sai Wan Memorial, Column 23

Rfm. B. Sheldon, age nk
Location of battle death nk, 1941/12/25
Stanley Military Cemetery, 5. B. Coll. Grave 1-4

Rfm. W.J. Smith, age nk
Stanley Mound, 1941/12/22
Sai Wan Memorial, Column 23

LCpl. R.d. Sommerville, age 21
Repulse Bay, 1941/12/23
Sai Wan Memorial, Column 23

Rfm. F. Sullivan, age nk
Stanley Mound, 1941/12/22
Sai Wan Memorial, Column 26

Rfm. H.A. Surette, age 35
Location of battle death nk, 1941/12/22
Sai Wan Cemetery, Grave #VIII. F. 11

Rfm. K.S.W. Swanson, age nk
Died of wounds, 1941/12/28
Stanley Military Cemetery, 5. B. Coll. Grave 1-4

Rfm. H.J. Tapp, age 33
Repulse Bay, 1941/12/20
Sai Wan Memorial, Column 26

Rfm. M.G.C. Thompson, age 18
Died of wounds, 1941/12/21
Sai Wan Cemetery, Grave #VIII. F. 18

Lieut, R.F. Thorn, age 25
Saddle between Stone Hill and Stanley Mound,
    1941/12/23
Sai Wan Memorial, Column 23

LCpl. C.W. Travers, age nk
Repulse Bay, 1941/12/23
Sai Wan Memorial, Column 23

Rfm. L.J. Trites, age 25
Bridge Hill, 1941/12/21
Sai Wan Memorial, Column 26

Rfm. L. Vigneault, age nk
Stanley View, near Water Tank, 1941/12/23
Sai Wan Memorial, Column 26

Rfm. R.L. Vincent, age 28
Location of battle death nk, 1941/12/23
Sai Wan Memorial, Column 23

Rfm. E.G. Watts, age nk
Repulse Bay Hotel, 1941/12/23
Sai Wan Memorial, Column 26

Lieut. G.M. Williams, age 38
Summit of Mount Parker, with Sgt Hughes,
    1941/12/19
Sai Wan Cemetery, Grave #VIII. G. 5

Rfm. J.H. Wills, age nk
Middle Gap, Black's Link, killed by LMG fire,
    1941/12/21
Sai Wan Cemetery, Grave #VIII. G. 6

Sgt. A. Wonnacott, age 40
Notting Hill, Repulse Bay?, 1941/12/22
Sai Wan Cemetery, Grave #VIII. G. 7

Lieut. A.R.. Woodside, age nk
Wong Nei Chong Gap, Brigade Headquarters,
    1941/12/23
Sai Wan Memorial, Column 23

The Winnipeg Grenadiers

Pte. H. Abgrall, age nk
Location of battle death nk, 1941/12/10
Sai Wan Memorial, Column 25

Cpl. T.G. Agerbak, age nk
Left wounded and killed with Mitchell's,
    1941/12/20
Sai Wan Memorial, Column 25

Pte. J.A. aitken, age 34
Jardine's Lookout, 1941/12/19
Sai Wan Memorial, Column 25

Pte. W.L. Atkinson, age nk
Mount Blount, 1941/12/19
Sai Wan Memorial, Column 25

Pte. E.H. Baptiste, age nk
Location of battle death nk, 1941/12/19
Sai Wan Memorial, Column 25

Pte. W.P. Barrett, age 24
Mount Cameron, 1941/12/25
Sai Wan Memorial, Column 25

Pte. O.A. Barron, age nk
Location of battle death nk, 1941/12/19
Sai Wan Memorial, Column 26

Cpl. C.M. Belz, age nk
Mount Butler, 1941/12/19
Sai Wan Memorial, Column 25

Lieut. G.A. Birkett, age nk
Summit of Jardine's Lookout, 1941/12/19
Sai Wan Memorial, Column 25

Pte. R. Blanchard, age nk
Bennet's Hill shelter, 1941/12/23
Sai Wan Cemetery, Grave #VIII. A. 12

Capt. A.S. Bowman, age 35
Wong Nei Chong Gap, killed in counter-attack
    ~0800hrs, 1941/12/19
Sai Wan Memorial, Column 23

LCpl. D.V. Boyd, age nk
Wong Nei Chong Gap, 1941/12/22
Sai Wan Memorial, Column 25

Pte. J. Brady, age 21
Black Hole, killed by shelling of, 1941/12/19
Sai Wan Memorial, Column 26

Pte. S.R. Carberry, age 20
Mount Blount, 1941/12/19
Sai Wan Cemetery, Grave #VIII. A. 17

Pte. W.T. Carcary, age 21
Stanley Village, 1941/12/24
Sai Wan Memorial, Column 26

Pte. G.J. Caswill, age 42
Magazine Gap, 1941/12/25
Sai Wan Memorial, Column 26

Pte. M. Chaboyer, age 25
Location of battle death nk, 1941/12/19
Sai Wan Memorial, Column 26

Pte. K.S. Cooper, age 20
Black's Link, 1941/12/21
Sai Wan Memorial, Column 26

Pte. W. Crawford, age nk
Last seen Mount Blount, 1941/12/10
Sai Wan Memorial, Column 26

2Liet. J.A.V. David, age 25
Shot in the head, 1941/12/21
Sai Wan Memorial, Column 25

Pte. A.H. Davis, age 38
Wong Nei Chong Gap, shot in the head,
    1941/12/19
Sai Wan Memorial, Column 26

Pte. L. Deslaurier, age nk
Stanley Gap, 1941/12/20
Sai Wan Memorial, Column 26

Pte. V.A. Donovan, age nk
Wong Nei Chong Gap, Brigade HQ, shot in
    the head, 1941/12/19
Sai Wan Memorial, Column 26

Pte. M.S. Dowswell, age 27
Wong Nei Chong Gap, 1941/12/22
Sai Wan Memorial, Column 26

Sgt. E.C. Dunsford, age 44
Mount Blount, 1941/12/19
Sai Wan Memorial, Column 25

Pte. N.C. Eccles, age 27
Black's Link, 1941/12/21
Sai Wan Memorial, Column 25

Pte. C.R. Edgely, age 40
Mount Nicholson, 1941/12/21
Sai Wan Memorial, Column 26

LSgt. C.E. Ferguson, age nk
Last seen Black's Link, 1941/12/21
Sai Wan Memorial, Column 25

Pte. D.H. Folster, age 19
Killed Wong Nei Chong Gap, 1941/12/19
Sai Wan Memorial, Column 26

Pte. H.T. Folster, age 25
Location of battlefield death nk, 1941/12/19
Sai Wan Memorial, Column 26

Pte. F.M. Foord, age 23
Mount Cameron, 1941/12/22
Sai Wan Memorial, Column 26

Sgt. R.M. Foster, age 27
Mount Nicholson, 1941/12/21
Sai Wan Memorial, Column 25

Lieut. C.D. French, age 20
Between Jardine's Lookout and Mount Butler,
    1941/12/19
Sai Wan Memorial, Column 26

Pte. D. Frobisher, age 27
Location of battle death nk, 1941/12/19
Sai Wan Memorial, Column 26

WO II W.B. Fryatt, age nk
Black's Link, 1941/1221
Sai Wan Memorial, Column 25

Pte. L. Gagne, age nk
Wong Nei Chong Gap, killed on road above
    Brigade HQ, 1941/12/19
Sai Wan Cemetery, Grave #IX. E. 6

Pte. V.E. Geekie, age 31
Jardine's Lookout, 1941/12/19
Sai Wan Memorial, Column 26

Pte. D. Girard, age nk
Location of battle death nk, 1941/12/21
Sai Wan Cemetery, Grave #VIII. B. 22

Pte. O. Goodman, age 22
Stanley Gap, 1941/1220
Sai Wan Memorial, Column 26

Pte. R.W. Grace, age nk
Location of battle death nk, 1941/12/19
Sai Wan Memorial, Column 26

Pte. A.A. Granger, age 17
Black Hole, probably murdered at, 1941/12/19
Sai Wan Memorial, Column 26

Pte. W.O. Grantham, age nk
Location of battle death nk, 1941/12/20
Sai Wan Memorial, Column 26

Pte. J.A. Gray, age 20
Missed last boat, believed murdered by
    Japanese, 1941/12/13
Sai Wan Memorial, Column 26

Cpl. A.R. Green, age 31
Died of wounds, 1941/12/24
Sai Wan Cemetery, Grave #VIII. B. 24

Maj. A.B. Gresham, age nk
Between Wong Nei Chong Gap and Mount
    Butler, 1941/12/19
Sai Wan Memorial, Column 23

Pte. H.L. Grierson, age nk
Last seen at Wong Nei Chong Gap, 1941/12/20
Sai Wan Memorial, Column 26

Pte. J.J. Gunn, age 24
Died of septic shrapnel wounds of back,
    buttock and scrotum, 1941/12/29
Sai Wan Cemetery, Grave #VIII. B. 25

Pte. L. McD. Hallett,, age nk
Jardine's Lookout, 1941/12/19
Sai Wan Memorial, Column 26

Pte. W.L. Hardisty, age 31
Repulse Bay, 1941/12/19
Sai Wan Memorial, Column 26

Pte. J. Hargraves, age 31
Location of battle death nk, 1941/12/22
Sai Wan Memorial, Column 26

Lieut. R.J. Hooper, age 26
Wong Nei Chong Gap, shot in chest by sniper,
    1941/12/21
Sai Wan Cemetery, Grave #VIII. C. 8

Pte. C.H.J. Johnson, age 33
Wong Nei Chong Gap, 1941/12/19 or
    1941/12/21
Sai Wan Memorial, Column 26

Sgt. H. Johnson, age nk
Mount Blount, 1941/12/19
Sai Wan Memorial, Column 25

Pte. L.W. Johnson, age 23
Mount Cameron, Chalk Trench, 1941/12/19
Sai Wan Memorial, Column 26

Pte. T. Jonsson, age 21
Mount Blount, 1941/12/19

Sai Wan Memorial, Column 26

Pte. M. Kasijan, age nk
Wan Chai Gap, 1941/12/22
Sai Wan Memorial, Column 26

Pte. W.A. Kellas, age 23
Jardine's Lookout, 1941/12/21
Sai Wan Memorial, Column 26

Pte. L.B.J. Kelly, age nk
Died in Hospital, 1941/12/25
Stanley Military Cemetery, 6. B. Coll. Grave 3-14

Cpl. H. Kelso, age 25
Wong Nei Chong Gap, 1941/12/19
Sai Wan Memorial, Column 25

Cpl. J.R. Kelso, age 21
Wong Nei Chong Gap, 1941/12/19
Sai Wan Memorial, Column 25

Pte. W.N. Kilfoyle, age 32
Murdered, a stomach wound too bad to march,
    1941/12/19
Sai Wan Memorial, Column 26

Pte. G.S. Land, age nk
Jardine's Lookout, bullet to head,
    1941/12/19
Sai Wan Memorial, Column 25

Pte. R.C. Land, age 21
Wong Nei Chong Gap AA position, bayoneted,
    1941/12/19
Sai Wan Memorial, Column 25

Pte. R.E.A. Larsen, age nk
Black's Link, 1941/12/21
Sai Wan Memorial, Column 26

Pte. G. Law, age 31
Mount Butler, 1941/12/19
Sai Wan Memorial, Column 26

Pte. K.R. Lawrie, nk
Mount Nicholson, 1941/12/21
Sai Wan Memorial, Column 26

Pte. F. Little, age nk
Mount Nicholson, 1941/12/21
Sai Wan Memorial, Column 26

Sgt. J. Long, age nk
Mount Cameron, killed by a shell,
    1941/12/22
Sai Wan Memorial, Column 25

Pte. E.J. Lousier, age 19
Wong Nei Chong Gap, 1941/12/19
Sai Wan Memorial, Column 26

Pte. J.A. Lowe, age 24
Jardine's Lookout, 1941/12/19
Sai Wan Memorial, Column 26

Pte. G.W. MacFarlane, age 40
Died in hospital, 1941/12/22
Stanley Military Cemetery, 6. A. Coll. Grave nk

Pte. J. Maltese, age nk
Location of battle death nk, 1941/12/25
Stanley Military Cemetery, 5. C. Coll. Grave
    4-20

Pte. T. Mattte, age 17
Last seen Mount Blount, 1941/12/20
Sai Wan Memorial, Column 26

Pte. D.C. Matthews, age 23
Ordnance House, road from golf course to
    Wong Nei Chong Gap, 1941/12/25
Sai Wan Cemetery, Grave #IX. D. 21

Pte. R.C. Maxwell, age nk
Wong Nei Chong Gap, 1941/12/19
Sai Wan Memorial, Column 26

Pte. W.F. McBride, age 29
Black's Link, 1941/12/21
Sai Wan Memorial, Column 26

Pte. M.S. McCorrister, age 20
Jardine's Lookout, 1941/12/19
Sai Wan Memorial, Column 26

Pte. R.C. McGowan, age nk
Wong Nei Chong Gap, 1941/12/19
Sai Wan Memorial, Column 26

Lieut. O.W. McKillop, age 33
Died of wounds, 1942/01/04
Sai Wan Cemetery, Grave #VIII. D. 23

Pte. R.A. Meades, age nk
Black's Link, Mount Cameron, 1941/12/21
Sai Wan Memorial, Column 26

Lieut. E.L. Mitchell, age 23
Murdered by Japanese, 1941/12/20
Sai Wan Cemetery, Grave #VIII. D. 13

Lieut. W.V. Mitchell, age 36
Murdered by Japanese, 1941/12/20
Sai Wan Memorial, Column 26

LCpl. A.W. Morgan, age 33
Mount Blount, 1941/12/21
Sai Wan Memorial, Column 25

Pte. J.I. Morris, age 23
Mount Blount, 1941/12/20
Sai Wan Memorial, Column 26

LCpl. D.J. O'Neill, age nk
Black Hole, murdered at, 1941/12/19
Sai Wan Memorial, Column 26

Pte. H. Orvis, age 22
Admitted Queen Mary Hospital on Dec 24,
    DOW, 1941/12/29
Sai Wan Memorial, Column 26

Pte. N.A. Osadchuk, age nk
Bayoneted near Wong Nei Cong GapAA
    position 41 Dec 19, 1941/12/23
Sai Wan Memorial, Column 26

WO II J.R. Osborn, age 42
Mount Butler, 1941/12/19
Sai Wan Memorial, Column 25

Pte. A.J. Ouelette, age 37
Location of battle death nk, 1941/12/25
Stanley Military Cemetery, 5. B. Coll. Grave 1-4

Pte. R. Owen, age 24
Wan Chai Gap, 1941/12/19
Sai Wan Memorial, Column 26

Pte. G.J. Pare, age 23
Wong Nei Chong Gap, killed on road above
    Brigade HQ, 1941/12/19
Sai Wan Memorial, Column 26

Pte. W.J. Parenteau, age nk
Location of battle death nk, 1941/12/19
Sai Wan Memorial, Column 26

Sgt. G.H. Paterson, age nk
Black's Link attacking the Wong Nei Chong
    Police Station, 1941/12/19
Sai Wan Memorial, Column 25

Pte. L. Pepin, age nk
Location of battle death nk, 1941/12/19
Sai Wan Memorial, Column 27

Pte. H. Piasta, age nk
Mount Cameron, 1941/12/22
Sai Wan Cemetery, Grave #VIII. E. 8

Pte. I.W. Pontius, age 22
Wong Nei Chong Gap, 1941/12/19
Sai Wan Memorial, Column 27

Pte. A. Poulsen, age 35
Wong Nei Chong Gap near AA Battery, Stanley
    Gap, 1941/12/19
Sai Wan Memorial, Column 27

Pte. W.A. Prieston, age nk
Killed Wong Nei Chong Gap, 1941/12/20
Sai Wan Memorial, Column 27

Pte. P. Procinsky, age nk
Black's Link, wounded on, 1941/12/20

Sai Wan Memorial, Column 27

Sgt. E.H. Rodgers, age 30
Location of battle death nk, 1941/12/21
Sai Wan Cemetery, Grave #VIII. E. 18

Pte. V. Ross, age nk
Magazine Gap, 1941/12/25
Sai Wan Memorial, Column 27

Pte. G.A. Rutherford, age 38
Repulse Bay, 1941/12/23
Sai Wan Cemetery, Grave #VIII. F. 2

Pte. H.E. Shatford, age nk
Mount Cameron, killed on Black's Link,
    1941/12/20
Sai Wan Memorial, Column 27

Pte. M. Shkolny, age nk
Jardine's Lookout, 1941/12/19
Sai Wan Memorial, Column 27

Pte. W.C. Shore, age nk
Location of battle death nk, 1941/12/23
Sai Wan Cemetery, Grave #VIII. E. 25

Pte. S. Silkey, age 35
Jardine's Lookout, 1941/12/19
Sai Wan Memorial, Column 27

Pte. K. Simpson, age nk
Jardine's Lookout, 1941/12/19
Sai Wan Memorial, Column 27

Pte. E.C. Smeltz, age 23
Bayoneted, 1941/12/20

Sai Wan Memorial, Column 27

Pte. C. Smith, age nk
Mount Butler, shot in forehead, 1941/12/19
Sai Wan Memorial, Column 25

Pte. C.E. Smith, age 21
Mount Blount, 1941/12/19
Sai Wan Memorial, Column 27

Pte. R.C. Smith, age 24
Location of battle death nk, 1941/12/ 19
Sai Wan Memorial, Column 26

Pte. W.J. Sprecht, age nk
Jardine's Lookout, 1941/12/19
Sai Wan Memorial, Column 28

Pte. E.G. Starrett, age 27
Wong Nei Chong Gap, 1941/12/19
Sai Wan Memorial, Column 25

Pte. W.J. Starrett, age 23
Black Hole, killed by shell at, 1941/12/20
Sai Wan Memorial, Column 25

Pte. S.F. Stodgell, age 22
Mount Blount, 1941/12/19
Sai Wan Memorial, Column 28

Pte. E. Swanson, age 34
Wong Nei Chong Gap, 1941/12/22
Sai Wan Memorial, Column 28

Capt. L.T. Tarbuth, age nk
Mount Butler/Jardine's Lookout boundary,
    1941/12/19

Sai Wan Memorial, Column 25

Pte. G. Teasdale, age 28
Mount Blount, killed at an artillery post near,
    1941/12/20
Sai Wan Memorial, Column 28

Pte. J.E. Tompkins, age nk
Location of battle death nk, 1941/12/19
Sai Wan Memorial, Column 28

Cpl. J.F. Vickers, age nk
Location of battle death nk, 1941/12/23
Sai Wan Memorial, Column 25

Pte. N.C. Walker, age nk
Black's Link, 1941/12/20
Sai Wan Memorial, Column 28

Pte. L.M. Warr, age nk
Admitted WNH Dec 23, 1941/12/24
Sai Wan Memorial, Column 25

Pte. B.B. Whalen, age 23
Bayoneted to death near Wong Nei Chong Gap
    AA position, 1941/12/19
Sai Wan Memorial, Column 28

Pte. T.C. White, age nk
Repulse Bay, 1941/12/22
Sai Wan Memorial, Column 28

Pte. E.E. Whiteside, age 26
Killed Wong Nei Chong Gap, 1941/12/20
Sai Wan Memorial, Column 28

Pte. H. Wiebe, age 19

Black's Link, 1941/12/21
Sai Wan Memorial, Column 28

Pte. J.G. Williams, age 36
Killed trying to carry Tarbruth to safety, Mount
    Blount, 1941/12/19
Sai Wan Memorial, Column 25

Pte. C. Willis, age nk
Black's Link, 1941/12/21
Sai Wan Memorial, Column 28

Pte. W.J. Wilson, age nk
Little Hong Kong, 1941/12/24
Sai Wan Memorial, Column 28

Pte. J. Wojnarsky, age 21
Died of wounds, 1942/01/07
Sai Wan Memorial, Column 28

LSgt. A.T. Woods, age nk
Middle Gap, Black's Link, by LMG fire,
    1941/12/21
Sai Wan Memorial, Column 25

Pte. F. Woytowich, age nk
Bennet's Hill Shelter, 1941/12/25
Sai Wan Cemetery, Grave #VIII. G. 8

Pte. R.F. Wright, age 23
Caroline Hill, killed attacking high ridge
    overlooking, 1941/12/19
Sai Wan Memorial, Column 28

Lieut. H.J. Young, age nk
Black's Link, 1941/12/21
Sai Wan Cemetery, Grave #VIII. G. 9

Courtesy of the Hong Kong Veterans'
    Commemorative Association

Notes

Introduction

1. Adolf Hitler became the leader of Germany in 1933. His government was strongly anti-democratic and emphasized obedience to the state. His Nazi Party promoted the idea that the German race was superior to all others and that "inferior" races, such as the Slavs of Eastern Europe or the Jews, should be enslaved or eliminated. Hitler was also determined to restore Germany's position in Europe, which had been severely weakened as a result of Germany's surrender to France, Britain, and the other victors after the First World War.

2. These oil reserves were located in the Dutch East Indies-Indonesia. Japan desperately required access to raw materials, such as oil, to support its industrialization and rearmament agenda.

3. After France's surrender to Germany, the country was divided in two parts — a German occupied northern and western zone, and an unoccupied southern zone known as Vichy France. The French government in Vichy was controlled by the Germans. The Germans eventually occupied Vichy France in November 1942.

Chapter 1: Bear on the Runway

1. Description of breed from *www.ukcdogs. com/WebSite.nsf/Breeds/Newfoundland*, accessed on December 29, 2008.

2. From *http://news.nationalgeographic.com/ news/2003/02/0207_030207_newfies.html*, accessed on December 29, 2008.

3. From *http://animalattraction.com/Re-sources/DogBreeds/Newfoundland*, accessed on January 4, 2008.

4. *Ibid.*

5. Steve Pitt, *The Day of the Flying Fox* (Toronto: Dundurn Press, 2008). The story of one particular Canadian Spitfire pilot.

6. Email from Eileen Elms of Gander, Newfoundland, December 27, 2008.

7. From *www.collectionscanada.gc.ca/conf-ederation/023001-2230-e.html*, accessed on December 29, 2008.

8. From *www.heritage.nf.ca/law/gander_base. html*, accessed on January 2, 2009.

9. Email from Eileen Elms, December 27, 2008.

10. From *www.cbc.ca/news/story/ 2000/08/11/ nf_gander000811.html*, accessed on January 2, 2009.

11. Email from Eileen Elms, December 27, 2008.

12. H.H. Herstein et al, *Challenge and Survival: The History of Canada* (Toronto: Prentice-Hall of Canada, 1970), 370.

13. From *www.collectionscanada.gc.ca/king/ 023011-1050.68-e.html*, accessed on December 29, 2008.

14. The British Commonwealth Air Training Plan was an aviation training program implemented during the Second World War, in-

volving Canada, Australia, the United Kingdom, New Zealand, and Southern Rhodesia. Its purpose was to train pilots, navigators, gunners, flight engineers, wireless operators, and bomb aimers for service in the Commonwealth Air Forces. Canada was considered an excellent location for the training program for a variety of reasons, including its ready supply of fuel and wide open flying spaces. Geographically, it was out of range of any threat from German or Japanese bombers or fighter planes and it occupied an excellent strategic location, almost equidistant, between the European and Pacific theatres. See *http://www.lancastermuseum.ca/bcatp. html*, accessed on May 25, 2009.

Chapter 2: Sergeant Gander, Royal Rifles of Canada

1. George MacDonell, *One Soldier's Story, 1939–1945* (Toronto: Dundurn Press, 2002), 47.
2. CBC Radio Broadcast, http://*archives.cbc. ca/war_conflict/veterans/topics/1039-5847/*, broadcast on August 11, 2000.
3. MacDonell, *One Soldier's Story, 1939–1945* (Toronto: Dundurn Press, 2002), 47.
4. Brereton Greenhous**,** *"C" Force to Hong Kong: A Canadian Catastrophe, 1941–1941* (Toronto: Dundurn Press, 1997), 10.
5. *Ibid.*, 10.
6. *Ibid.*, 11.
7. *Ibid.*, 17.
8. *Ibid.*, 21.
9. *Ibid.*, 18. Major-General Crerar was chief of the Canadian general staff in 1941. Historians disagree over the extent of his culpability for sending the Royal Rifles and the Winnipeg Grenadiers to Hong Kong, but he did

advise Prime Minister Mackenzie King that there was "no military risk" in sending the Canadian troops to Hong Kong.
10. Greenhous, *"C" Force to Hong Kong: A Canadian Catastrophe, 1941–1941* (Toronto: Dundurn Press, 1997), 22.
11. From *www.hkvca.ca/historical/accounts/ williambell/chapter1.htm*, accessed on December 3, 2008.
12. Oliver Lindsay, *The Lasting Honour: The Fall of Hong Kong, 1941* (London: Hamish Hamilton, 1978), 8.
13. The Washington Naval Conferences were organized by American President Warren Harding's administration and were held in Washington D.C. from November 12, 1921, to February 6, 1922. They were attended by nine nations who had interests in the Pacific Ocean and East Asia. One of the primary goals was to encourage disarmament and peace in the region, and to limit the building of new battleship fleets.
14. Communism is an authoritarian system of government where the state plans and controls the economy. This system of government was established in Russia (Soviet Union) following the October Revolution in 1917, with the state taking ownership of all personal property.
15. Hong Kong Veterans Commemorative Association, *The Royal Rifles of Canada in Hong Kong: 1941–1945* (Carp, ON: Baird O'Keefe Publishing Inc., 2001), 25.
16. From *http://avalon.law.yale.edu/wwii/tri-parti.asp*, accessed on December 29, 2008.
17. Walter Lord, *The Miracle of Dunkirk* (New York: Viking Press, 1982), 286. The evacuation from Dunkirk took place over

nine days, from May 26 to June 4, 1940. Hundreds of ships, including Royal Navy vessels, fishing boats, pleasure craft, and commercial vessels, travelled across the English Channel, from Britain, to evacuate the British and French forces that had been forced back onto the beaches by the advancing Germans. A Canadian, Commander James Campbell Clouston, who was serving with the Royal Navy, was assigned the role of pier master of the Eastern Mole. The Eastern Mole was a breakwater that formed the entrance to Dunkirk's harbour. Ships were brought up alongside and Clouston lined the retreating soldiers up, in an orderly fashion, and at one point was disembarking over 2,000 men an hour. He served as pier master for five nights, evacuating over one hundred thousand men.

Chapter 3: Mascot on the Move

1. From *www.geocities.com/phil_doddrige/*, accessed on December 3, 2008.
2. MacDonell, *One Soldier's Story, 1939–1945* (Toronto: Dundurn Press, 2002), 49.
3. *Ibid.*, 49.
4. Carl Vincent, *No Reason Why* (Stittsville, ON: Canada's Wings Inc., 1981), 109. The Canadian Postal Corps was an administrative corps of the Canadian Army.
5. Brereton Greenhous, *"C" Force to Hong Kong: A Canadian Catastrophe, 1941–1945* (Toronto: Dundurn Press, 1997), 28.
6. *Ibid.*, 29.
7. *Ibid.*, 32.
8. *Ibid.*, 32.
9. Carl Vincent, *No Reason Why* (Stittsville, ON: Canada's Wings Inc., 1981), 109.

Chapter 4: The Calm Before the Storm

1. In 1984, an agreement signed by Great Britain and China decreed that the sovereignty of Hong Kong would revert back to China in 1997. Since 1997 Hong Kong has been a Special Administrative Region of the People's Republic of China. It is largely autonomous of China, except in foreign and defence affairs.
2. Carl Vincent, *No Reason Why* (Stittsville, ON: Canada's Wings Inc., 1981), 6.
3. Hong Kong Veterans' Association, *The Royal Rifles of Canada in Hong Kong: 1941–1945* (Carp, ON: Baird O'Keefe Publishing Inc., 2001), 24.
4. Carl Vincent, *No Reason Why*, 6.
5. From *www.hkvca.ca/historical/accounts/cadoret.htm*, accessed on December 3, 2008.
6. Brereton Greenhous, *"C" Force to Hong Kong: A Canadian Catastrophe, 1941–1945*: 35.
7. *Ibid.*, 35.
8. Carl Vincent, *No Reason Why* (Stittsville, ON: Canada's Wings Inc., 1981), 109.
9. Oliver Lindsay, *The Lasting Honour: The Fall of Hong Kong, 1941* (London: Hamish Hamilton, 1978), 17.
10. Interview with Rifleman John Beebe, available at *www.geocities.com/rcwpca/index-8.html*, accessed on December 3, 2008.
11. Ted Ferguson, *Desperate Siege: The Battle of Hong Kong* (Toronto: Doubleday Canada Ltd., 1980), ix.
12. Hong Kong Veterans Commemorative Association, *The Royal Rifles of Canada in Hong Kong: 1941–1945* (Carp, ON: Baird O'Keefe Publishing Inc., 2001), 15.
13. Terrence and Brian McKenna, *The Valour*

and the Horror: Savage Christmas Hong Kong 1941, CBC Television, 1992.

14. *Ibid.*

15. MacDonell, *One Soldier's Story, 1939–1945* (Toronto: Dundurn Press, 2002), 48.

16. CBC Radio Broadcast, available at *http://archives.cbc.ca/war_conflict/veterans/topics/1039-5847/*, broadcast on August 11, 2000.

17. Ted Ferguson, *Desperate Siege: The Battle of Hong Kong* (Toronto: Doubleday Canada Ltd., 1980), ix.

18. Regimental war diaries are notes written as events happen, often quickly jotted with no time for reflection. The War Diary of the Royal Rifles is held by the Canadian Department of Defence/Directorate of History.

19. Hong Kong Veterans Commemorative Association, *The Royal Rifles of Canada in Hong Kong: 1941–1945* (Carp, ON: Baird O'Keefe Publishing Inc., 2001),16.

20. *Ibid.*, 43.

21. *Ibid.*

20. *Ibid.*

Chapter 5: The Battle Rages

1. The American naval base at Pearl Harbor, Hawaii, was the target of a surprise attack conducted by the Japanese navy on December 7, 1941. The attack was conducted before a formal declaration of war by Japan. This act brought the United States into the Second World War.

2. Ted Ferguson, *Desperate Siege: The Battle of Hong Kong* (Toronto: Doubleday Canada Ltd., 1980), 45.

3. Hong Kong Veterans Commemorative Association, *The Royal Rifles of Canada in Hong Kong: 1941–1945* (Carp, ON: Baird O'Keefe Publishing Inc., 2001), 45.

4. *Ibid.*, 36.

5. *Ibid.*, 52.

6. *Ibid.*, 53.

7. *Ibid.*, 52.

8. *Ibid.*, 54.

9. *Ibid.*, 54.

10. Brereton Greenhous, *"C" Force to Hong Kong: A Canadian Catastrophe, 1941–1941* (Toronto: Dundurn Press, 1997), 69.

11. *Ibid.*, 69.

12. Excerpt from Rifleman Sydney Skelton's diary, available at *www.geocities.com/rcwpca/index-13.html*, accessed on December 4, 2008.

13. Isabel George, "Dog of War," *Companions Magazine*, Issue 16 (Spring 2001), 31.

14. Hong Kong Veterans Commemorative Association, *The Royal Rifles of Canada in Hong Kong: 1941–1945* (Carp, ON: Baird O'Keefe Publishing Inc., 2001), 61.

15. CBC Radio Broadcast, available at *http://archives.cbc.ca/war_conflict/veterans/topics/1039-5847/*, broadcast on August 11, 2000.

16. Brereton Greenhous, *"C" Force to Hong Kong: A Canadian Catastrophe, 1941–1941* (Toronto: Dundurn Press, 1997), 75.

17. Isabel George, "Dog of War," *Companions Magazine*, Issue 16 (Spring 2001), 31.

18. *Ibid.*, 31.

19. Tony Banham, *Not the Slightest Chance: The Defence of Hong Kong, 1941* (Hong Kong: Hong Kong University Press, 2003), 114.

20. CBC Radio Broadcast, available at *http://archives.cbc.ca/war_conflict/veterans/*

topics/1039-5847/, broadcast on August 11, 2000.

21. *Ibid.*
22. *Ibid.*
23. Brereton Greenhous, *"C" Force to Hong Kong: A Canadian Catastrophe, 1941–1941* (Toronto: Dundurn Press, 1997), 97.
24. *Ibid.*, 97.
25. *Ibid.*, 98.
26. MacDonell, *One Soldier's Story, 1939–1945* (Toronto: Dundurn Press, 2002), 48.
27. The Geneva Convention of 1929 was drawn up by the International Committee of the Red Cross specifically to address the treatment of prisoners of war. Geneva Conventions and their amendments are international treaties that outline the rules limiting the barbarity of war. They protect non combatants (i.e., civilians, medics) and those who are no longer able to fight (i.e., wounded, prisoners), and are universally accepted. They are a cornerstone of international humanitarian law and have currently been ratified by 194 countries. See *www.icrc.org/Web/Eng/siteeng0.nsf/htmlall/genevaconventions*, accessed on May 25, 2009.
28. Brereton Greenhous, *"C" Force to Hong Kong: A Canadian Catastrophe, 1941–1941* (Toronto: Dundurn Press, 1997), 75.
29. Carl Vincent, *No Reason Why* (Stittsville, ON: Canada's Wings Inc., 1981), 211.
30. Brereton Greenhous, *"C" Force to Hong Kong: A Canadian Catastrophe, 1941–1941* (Toronto: Dundurn Press, 1997), 118.
31. Carl Vincent, *No Reason Why* (Stittsville, ON: Canada's Wings Inc., 1981), 214.

Chapter 6: Gander Gets His Medal

1. From *www.hkvca.ca/aboutus/hkvahist.htm*, accessed on January 3, 2009.
2. *Ibid.*
3. From *www.pdsa.org.uk/mariadickin.html*, accessed on January 3, 2009.
4. *Ibid.*
5. From *www.pdsa.org.uk/dickinmedal.html*, accessed on January 2, 2009.
6. Isabel George, "Dog of War," *Companions Magazine*, Issue 16 (Spring 2001), 32.
7. "Heroic Dog of Hong Kong Recognized," *Legion Magazine*, January 11, 2001.
8. Isabel George, "Dog of War," *Companions Magazine*, Issue 16 (Spring 2001), 32.
9. Buzz Bourdon, "Dog's War Medal Praised as One of 'Most Deserving'," The *Ottawa Citizen*, October 28, 2000.

Chapter 7: Animals at War

1. From *http://news.bbc.co.uk/2/hi/uk_news/4037873.stm*, accessed on January 4, 2009.
2. Val Shushkewich, *The Real Winnie: A One-of-a-Kind Bear* (Toronto: Natural Heritage Books, 2003), 22.
3. From *www.vac-acc.gc.ca/youth/sub.cfm?source=feature/week2006/vw_edres/animalswar_news/page5*, accessed on December 18, 2008.
4. *Ibid.*
5. Evelyn Le Chene, *Silent Heroes: The Bravery and Devotion of Animals in War* (London: Souvenir Press, 1994), 96.

Bibliography

Articles

Bourden, Buzz. "Dog's War Medal Praised as One of 'Most Deserving'." *Ottawa Citizen*, October 28, 2000.

Dick, Ray. "Heroic Newfoundland Dog Awarded Animal VC." *Legion Magazine* (November/December 2000), 56.

George, Isabel. "Dog of War." *Companions*, Issue 16, (Spring 2001), 30–32.

Books

Axelrod, Alan. *Encyclopedia of World War II.* NewYork: Facts on File, 2007.

Cambon, Ken. *Guest of Hirohito.* Vancouver: PW Press, 1990.

Carew, Tim. *The Fall of Hong Kong.* London: Blond, 1960.

Banham, Tony. *Not the Slightest Chance: The Defence of Hong Kong, 1941.* Hong Kong: Hong Kong University Press, 2003.

Ferguson, Ted. *Desperate Siege: The Battle of Hong Kong.* Toronto: Doubleday Canada Ltd., 1980.

George, Isabel, et al. *Animals at War.* London: Usborne Publishing, 2006.

Greenhous, Brereton. *"C" Force to Hong Kong: A Canadian Catastrophe, 1941–1945.* Toronto: Dundurn Press, 1997.

Herstein, H.H., et al. *Challenge and Survival: The History of Canada.* Toronto: Prentice-Hall of Canada, 1970.

Hong Kong Veterans' Association. *The Royal Rifles of Canada in Hong Kong: 1941–1945.* Carp, ON: Baird O'Keefe Publishing Co., 2001.

Le Chene, Evelyn. *Silent Heroes: The Bravery and Devotion of Animals in War.* London: Souvenir Press, 1994.

Lewis, Val. *Ships' Cats in War and Peace.* Middlesex: Nauticalia Ltd., 2001.

Lindsay, Oliver. *The Lasting Honour: The Fall of Hong Kong, 1941.* London: Hamish Hamilton, 1978.

Lord, Walter. *The Miracle of Dunkirk.* New York: Viking Press, 1982.

MacDonell, George. *One Soldier's Story, 1939–1945.* Toronto: Dundurn Press, 2002.

Veterans Affairs Canada. *Canadians in Hong Kong.* Ottawa: Veterans Affairs Canada, 2005.

Vincent, Carl. *No Reason Why: The Canadian Hong Kong Tragedy.* Stittsville, ON: Canada's Wings Inc., 1981.

Videos

McKenna, Brian and Terrence (writers), "Savage Christmas: Hong Kong 1941," Television Documentary: *The Valour and the Horror.* Story by D'Arcy O'Connor, National Film Board of Canada, 1992.

Websites (accessed over 2008–09)

"Animal Attraction." *http://animalattraction. com/*.

"Hong Kong Veterans Award Bravery Medal to Dog." *http://archives.cbc.ca/war_conflict/ veterans/clips/5847/*.

"Canine War Hero." *www.cbc.ca/news/story/ 2000/08/11/nf_gander000811.html*.

"Major Maurice A. Parker." *www.geocities.com/ rcwpca/index.html*.

"HMCS *Prince Robert* Tribute." *http:// airmuseum.ca/rcn/prsellers.html*.

"Hong Kong Veterans' Commemorative Association." *www.hkvca.ca*.

"International Committee of the Red Cross." *www.icrc.org/Web/Eng/siteeng0.nsf/html/ genevaconventions*.

"Library and Archives Canada." *http:// collectionscanada.gc.ca/*.

"The British Commonwealth Air Training Plan." *www.lancastermuseum.ca/bcatp.html*.

"Guard Dogs: Newfoundlands' Lifesaving Past, Present." *http://news.nationalgeographic. com/news/2003/02/0207_030207_newfies. html*.

"Newfound Friends." *www.newfoundfriends. co.uk/*.

"Newfoundland/Labrador Heritage." *www.heri- tage.nf.ca*.

"North Atlantic Aviation Museum." *www. naam.ca*.

"People's Dispensary for Sick Animals." *www. pdsa.org.uk*.

"Purr-n-Fur UK." *www.purr-n-fur.org.uk*.

"United Kennel Club." *www.ukcdogs.com*.

"Veterans Affairs Canada." *www.vac-acc.gc.ca*.

Other Sources

Email correspondence with Eileen Elms, former Gander playmate, October to December 2008.

Email correspondence with Isabel George, PDSA, 2008–09.

Email correspondence with Derrill Henderson, President HKVCA, 2008.

Email correspondence with Ron Parker, son of Major Maurice Parker of the Royal Rifles, 2007–08.

Interview and emails with Jeremey Swanson, former Canadian War Museum Commemorations Officer, 2006–08.

Email correspondence with Jim Trick, Secretary HKVCA, 2007–08.

Index

Lyndon, Major C.A. (WG), 44, 45

M
MacDonell, Sergeant George (RRC), 30, 31, 40, 54, 70
Maltby, Major General C.M., 50, 54, 60
Manchester, Sergeant Bob (WG), 10, 12
Mainland Brigade, 54, 55
Maquis, DM, 106
Mary of Exeter, DM, 92, 106, 107
McCrae, Doctor/Lieutenant Colonel John, 89, 90
Mercury, DM, 107
Middlesex Regiment, 1st Battalion, 50, 56, 58
Milne, Christopher Robin, 89
Montreal, 23
Murphy, the donkey, 82–84

N
Navy Blue, DM, 104
Newfoundland, Dominion of, 17, 20–22, 75
New Territories, Hong Kong, 46, 47, 55, 56, 60
Niimi, Vice Admiral Masaichi, 61
North Point Camp, 68

O
Olga, DM, 108
Osborn, Sergeant Major John, VC, 10, 72, 73, 74, 96

P
Paddy, DM, 104
Pal, 17, 20, 24, 25, *see also* Gander
Pat (Prime Minister Mackenzie King's dog), 27
Pearl Harbor, 45, 59
People's Dispensary for Sick Animals (PDSA), 11, 75–78, 80, 85

Peter, DM, 99, 100
Phillips, Rear Admiral Tom, 32
Pigeon DD.43.Q.879, DM, 108
Pigeon DD.43.T.139, DM, 108
Pigeon NPS.42.NS.2780, DM, 106
Pigeon NPS.42.NS.7524, DM, 106
Pigeon NURP.38.BPC.6, DM, 107
Pigeon NURP.43.CC.1418, DM, 107
Princess, DM, 107
Prisoner of War (POW) Camps, 15, 68, 70
Punch and Judy, DM, 99, 100
Punjabis, 2/14th, 50, 55, 58, 60

Q
Quebec City, 30, 39, 40
Queenie (Winnipeg Grenadier dog), 33

R
Rajputs, 5/7th, 50, 55, 58, 61
Ratcliffe, Mike, 25
Regal, DM, 109
Rex, DM, 99
Ricky, DM, 100, 101
Rifleman Khan, DM, 98
Rimouski, Quebec, 23
Rip, DM, 98, 99
Rob, DM, 97
Roosevelt, President Franklin Delano, 27, 35
Royal Air Force (RAF), 17, 23, 28, 37, 51, 60
Royal Artillery, 49
Royal Blue, DM, 105
Royal Canadian Air Force (RCAF), 20, 23, 28
Royal Engineers, 49
Royal Navy, 37, 46, 49, 51, 68
Royal Rifles of Canada, 11, 15, 26, 30, 31, 33, 37, 38, 40–42, 48, 54–62, 65, 66, 68, 73, 74, 78, *see also* Appendix B and C

About the Author

Robyn Walker was born and raised in St. Thomas, Ontario. She received a Specialized Honours degree in History from the University of Guelph, a Masters in Library and Information Science from the University of Western Ontario, and a Bachelor of Education from St. Francis Xavier University. Researching various aspects of military history has long been a personal interest and while conducting the research for her article about Simon of the *Amethyst* (a cat who was awarded the PDSA Dickin Medal for bravery during the Yangtze Incident) Robyn was surprised to discover that a Canadian dog had been awarded the medal as well. Intrigued by this little known and unique Canadian story, she was inspired to write about this incredible dog's heroic tale. Robyn currently works as a school librarian and freelance writer. Her work has appeared in *Cat Fancy* and *The School Library Journal*, and she is currently awaiting publication of her second book on female spies of the Second World War. Robyn is a regular book reviewer for *The School Library Journal*. She lives in St. Thomas with her husband, Terry, son, Jed, and a houseful of much-loved pets.

Courtesy of Colledge Studios.

Of Related Interest

The Real Winnie
A One-of-a-Kind Bear
by Val Shushkewich
978-1- 89621-989-9 / $16.95

The story of Winnie, the real Canadian bear that captured the heart of Christopher, son of A.A. Milne, and became immortalized in the Winnie the Pooh stories, is told against the backdrop of the First World War. In August 1914, a Canadian soldier and veterinarian named Lieutenant Harry Colebourn, en route to a training camp in Quebec, purchased a black bear cub in White River, Ontario, which he named Winnipeg.

First a regimental mascot for Canadians training for wartime service, Winnie then became a star attraction at the London Zoo, and ultimately inspired one of the best-loved characters in children's literature. For those many generations of readers who adored Winnie the Pooh, and for those intrigued by the unique stories embedded in Canadian history, this book is a feast of information about a one-of-a-kind bear set during a poignant period of world history.

Day of the Flying Fox
The True Story of World War II Pilot Charley Fox
by Steve Pitt
978-1- 55002-808-9 / $19.99

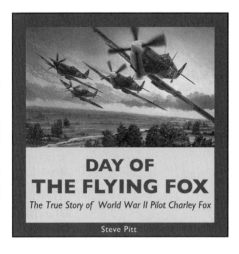

Canadian World War II pilot Charley Fox, now in his late eighties, has had a thrilling life, especially on the day in July 1944 in France when he spotted a black staff car, the kind usually employed to drive high-ranking Third Reich dignitaries. Already noted for his skill in dive-bombing and strafing the enemy, Fox went in to attack the automobile. As it turned out, the car contained famed German General Erwin Rommel, the Desert Fox, and Charley succeeded in wounding him.

Author Steve Pitt focuses on this seminal event in Charley Fox's life and in the war, but he also provides fascinating aspects of the period, including profiles of noted ace pilots Buzz Beurling and Billy Bishop, Jr., and Great Escape architect Walter Floody, as well as sidebars about Hurricanes, Spitfires, and Messerschmitts.

True Stories of Rescue and Survival
Canada's Unknown Heroes
by Carolyn Matthews
978-1- 55002-851-5 / $19.99

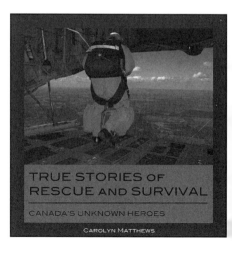

A crab boat off Newfoundland catches fire, and a rescue is undertaken by helicopter. A child goes missing in a New Brunswick forest, and a desperate hunt is mounted. A climber falls on a British Columbia mountain, and a helicopter rescue is attempted. A civilian chopper crashes in Nunavut, and a search-and-rescue team braves a savage snowstorm to find survivors.

True Stories of Rescue and Survival features those true stories and many more from across the country, past and present. Its heroes are to be found in the RCMP, city police forces, the Canadian military, and among all the rescue workers and specialists of the Canadian Coast Guard.

DUNDURN PRESS
www.dundurn.com

Available at your favourite bookseller

Tell us your story! What did you think of this book? Join the conversation at www.definingcanada.ca/tell-your-story by telling us what you think.

Marquis Book Printing Inc.

Québec, Canada
2009

282-3